11/06

Grey's Essential Miscellany for Teachers

Related Titles:

Devil's Dictionary of Education – Tyrrell Burgess
100 Essential Lists for Teachers – Duncan Grey

GREY'S ESSENTIAL MISCELLANY FOR TEACHERS

Duncan Grey

continuum
LONDON • NEW YORK

*For my colleagues at
Netherhall and Hinchingbrooke Schools.*

In memory of Alfred Pearse and the mainly anonymous
illustrators of the *Boy's Own Paper* 1890–1930.

Continuum International Publishing Group

The Tower Building   15 East 26th Street
11 York Road   New York, NY 10010
London
SE1 7NX

www.continuumbooks.com

British Library Cataloguing-in-Publication Data
A catalogue record for this book is available from the British
Library.

ISBN: 0 8264 7491 8 (hardback)

Typeset by Ben Cracknell Studios
Printed and bound in Great Britain by MPG Books Ltd,
Bodmin, Cornwall

CONTENTS

INTRODUCTION

This is intended as a loose collection of facts, information and thoughts that could:

  inform an educational discussion and/or
  raise an intrigued eyebrow in the staffroom;
  confirm or (perish the thought) challenge prejudices and opinion.

It could be 'Well I never!' or 'Strange but true' or 'I always thought that too and here's great evidence', and some might even make it to the staffroom noticeboard.

If there is any subversive element, that only confirms my view that any teacher who has survived ROSLA and the Work Related Curriculum, GCE CSE and GCSE, the National Curriculum and a succession of education ministers has a lot to be sceptical or even cynical about.

Although every effort has been made to verify information and statistics given here, the responsibility remains with the author. (Statistics apply to England and Wales unless stated otherwise.) On the other hand the only way to confirm, explain or expand upon the information is to visit the source, which is given as far as possible. And that's part of the purpose of this *Miscellany* – to stimulate you to ask why and find out more for yourself. Which is what education *should* be all about.

So you want to teach?

Wilfred Owen in a letter to his mother (1910) wrote that his former headmaster's wife had called:

> to warn me against the Teaching Profession. Her husband could not candidly do this she said, but she thinks it 'wicked' that young people should enter it without a fair premonition of the hopelessness of their fate, and without knowing of the profound dissatisfaction among all who are now teachers.

A good teacher ...

is kind
is generous
listens to you
encourages you
has faith in you
keeps confidences
likes teaching children
likes teaching their subject
takes time to explain things
helps you when you're stuck

tells you how you are doing
allows you to have your say
doesn't give up on you
cares for your opinion
makes you feel clever
treats people equally
stands up for you
makes allowances
tells the truth
is forgiving.

Descriptions by Year 8 pupils, quoted in the McBer Report (2000)

Effective teachers will ...

- need to deal with continual change;
- harness distance learning and new media;
- work in a school that must foster continuous improvement;
- be open to integrate good practice from other teachers, schools, countries;
- value genuine team working;
- appreciate mutual feedback – through lesson observation or other means – as an essential part of professional development.

Quoted in the McBer Report (2000)

What are the seven teaching skills?

The Ofsted inspection headings

High expectations
Planning
Methods and strategies
Pupil management, discipline
Time and resource management
Assessment
Homework, relating to:
    Time on task
    Lesson flow.

Head counting

General teacher numbers 2003
(Full-time equivalent regular teachers in
the maintained schools sector in England)

January 2004: 427,800 (highest for more than 20 years)
January 2003: 423,600
    A rise of: 4,000 (1 per cent) since January 2002,
                13,400 since January 2001,
                25,900 since 1998.
Occasional (short-term supply) teachers went down by 2,700
to 14,800.

Nursery and primary phase:
- Regular teachers remained at 197,400.
- Occasional teachers fell by 1,700 to 8,400.
- The total of teachers fell by 1,700 to 205,800.

Secondary phase:
- Regular teachers rose by 3,700 to 206,900.
- Occasional teachers fell by 900 to 5,500.
- The total of teachers rose by 2,800 to 212,400.

DfES statistical website: http://www.dfes.gov.uk/statistics/

The spinster teacher and the disappearing male

Until the Second World War it was forbidden for female teachers to be married. Virtually all women teachers were in the primary sector.

The 1944 Butler Education Act raised the school leaving age to 15 and lifted the ban on women teachers marrying.

The decline in number of male secondary teachers began in 1944 and continued generally to fall throughout the 1980s and 1990s.

Technicians

Secondary schools have had technicians in laboratories, Design Technology departments and IT rooms for many years, but they were rare in primary schools – until the advent of ICT.

The number of full-time equivalent technicians in primary schools rose from 19.6 in 2001 to 920.9 in 2003.

DfES (2003a)

Non-teaching staff

Full-time equivalent staff (includes teaching assistants, technicians and other non-administrative staff):

Primary:	1996 50,600	2001	83,100
Secondary:	1996 23,100	2001	37,300.

Total (nursery, primary, secondary, special schools and pupil referral units):

2003: 225,400
1998: 144,000.

Increase in non-teaching staff providing additional classroom learning support: 1996–2001: 56 per cent.

Social Trends 32: http://www.statistics.gov.uk; DfES (2003a)

New public sector jobs

Half a million new public sector jobs have been created since 1997:

classroom assistants:	90,000
teachers:	20,000
nurses:	50,000
doctors:	c. 20,000
policemen:	10,000.

From Hansard, quoted in The Times, *13 February 2004*

What do teaching assistants do?

	Primary %	Secondary %
Work with groups of specified pupils	97	89
Work with individual specified pupils	91	95
Photocopying	93	79
Construct displays	88	40
First aid/Administer medicine	76	21
Playground duty	74	14
Team teach whole class	72	41
Ordering stock and resources	41	30
Pursuing absences	23	26

NFER research

Do teachers suffer from low morale?

Number of teachers in England participating in the teacher 'census': 70,011.

Number claiming their morale was lower than when they joined the profession: 56 per cent.

General Teaching Council estimate of teachers who will leave the profession within five years for a job outside education: 28,500.

Number of places on teacher training courses in England in 2004/5 to be funded by the Department for Education and Skills: 35,800.

GTC 'census' 2002–3

Main factors that demotivate teachers

- workload (including unnecessary paperwork): 56 per cent
- initiative overload: 39 per cent
- target-driven culture: 35 per cent
- poor pupil behaviour and discipline: 31 per cent.

Number of teachers who feel respected by their colleagues: > 90 per cent.

Number who believe the media gives them no or little respect: 86 per cent.

Number who believe the government gives them no or little respect: 78 per cent.

Number who 'strongly agree' that most members of the public do not understand the nature and complexity of the teacher's job: 74 per cent.

GTC 'census' 2002–3

Conflict at work

The Teacher Support Network reported that conflict with colleagues and bullying by managers accounted for more than twice as many contacts to them as pupil misbehaviour.

Over four years, 76,000 teachers (30,000 in 2003) contacted the Network. Stress, anxiety and depression accounted for the highest number of calls:

Conflict: 10.2 per cent

Workload/hours: 4.8 per cent

Pupil behaviour: 4.3 per cent

Long-term sick leave: 4.2 per cent.

When did you last give yourself a skills audit?

Consider your skills in:

Communication	The ability to communicate effectively in a variety of ways – writing, speaking, describing, individually, in small and large groups.

IT	Practical skills, the ability to use IT effectively in a variety of circumstances, skills of teaching others how to make use of IT.
People skills	Dealing with pupils, parents, agencies; the ability to relate sensitively to people; counselling skills.
Management of people	The ability to work with people in a team; working together; encouraging others to work in a common direction.
Management of change	The ability to plan and to carry out a plan – for yourself and for others. Teachers have experienced more change than most professions in recent years – how did you cope?
Literacy and numeracy	Almost by definition you have these, but how well can you express yourself in writing and in speaking; can you interpret statistics or simplify things for others?
Subject-specific skills for industry	Languages, science-based experience, business related, writing …
Learning and training skills	Training is a different skill from teaching but much in demand; can you show that you are able and willing to learn new skills and adapt to new challenges and new environments?
Flexibility	Can you adapt – and are you willing to be flexible? How do you react when a change of classroom, syllabus or working practice is called for?
Motivation	Self-motivation; the ability to carry through a mission.
Independent working	Independence of thought and action; the ability to decide when to work alone and when in a team; being trusted.

Going for a different job?

All of the above are required skills for many jobs outside of the classroom. Skilled communicators are required everywhere.

Teachers often have a number of the above skills by virtue of their qualifications and experience in schools.

Try to find good examples of each of these skills from your recent experience and refer to them in your CV or job application.

Former teachers

Billy Crystal, Sebastian Faulks, Bryan Ferry, Dawn French, Duncan Grey, Nick Hancock, Sarah Kennedy, Luciano Pavarotti, Anita Roddick, Sting.

Recruitment

Recruitment to teacher training fell for eight years in a row from 1992/3, but has now risen for three successive years:

- Increase in full-time teachers with a degree: 12 per cent.
- Increase in subject periods taught by full-time teachers with a degree in these subjects: 8 per cent.
- Increase in full-time teachers teaching subjects with a degree in these subjects: 4 per cent.
- Increase in teachers teaching Maths without a post-A-level in that subject: 2 per cent.

DfES (2003b)

Heroes of 'The Battle with 5B'

Despite the frequent appearance of a well-deserved MBE for a road-crossing supervisor or a caretaker, the Honours Lists of those receiving awards and medals for service to the country are inclined towards civil servants.

What are the odds on your receiving an Honour?

- Diplomat: 1 in 123.
- Teacher: 1 in 15,500.
- Nurse: 1 in 20,000.

There are, of course, secret initiation ceremonies to be undergone

Teachers' reports now the length of novels

The *Daily Telegraph* noted that teachers are having to write 'reports the size of novels' alongside test scores for five-year-olds.

The Qualifications and Curriculum Authority requires teachers to record 117 individual judgements, backed up by evidence, on each child.

These assessments amount to a total of 105,300 words for a class of 30, longer than Milton's *Paradise Lost* (90,382 words) and rivalling Homer's *Iliad* (138,044 words).

The Daily Telegraph, *21 June 2004*

Shortage of cash?

It's in the post ...

Forecast increase in education spending: to rise to 5.6 per cent of GDP by 2005/6.

Spending will rise by an average of 6 per cent a year in real terms over the next three years, to £57.8 billion in 2005/6.

Payments directly to schools will be at least £165,000 for a typical secondary school, and £50,000 for a primary school: increases of £50,000 and £10,000 respectively.

Spending Review UK 2003

Past education spending

(Historical expenditure on education in the UK in £billions in real terms)

1993–4	40.5	1998–9	41.9
1994–5	41.9	1999–2000	42.9
1995–6	41.7	2000–1	45.3
1996–7	41.4	2001–2	49.4
1997–8	41.3	2002–3	52.0 (estimated)

Education spending in other countries

(Percentage of GNP spent on education)

New Caledonia	13.5
St Lucia	9.8
UK	5.3
USA	5.4
Nigeria	0.7
Somalia	0.4

Can you afford a home?

A 2003 Halifax Bank survey showed that the average cost of a London home was 6.5 times the average teacher's salary.

Raise money – sell fields

Number of applications to build on sports fields:

1999–2000: 625
2002–2003: 1,325

How much does a school cost?

DfES guidance on secondary school building costs for 2002 says the average total cost of building a new secondary school should be around £14.6 million.

Raise money – sell qualifications

British university with branch in Israeli petrol station 'issued 5,500 bogus degrees'

5,500 people paid for fictitious qualifications from a British university. An Israeli police spokesman said, 'Anywhere that was big enough to hold a desk and a chair, including in one case a petrol station, became a branch of the University of H_____.'

Teachers' pay compared …

England, Wales and Northern Ireland 2003

Teachers	£
Head	35,544–88,155+
Advanced skills teacher	29,757–47,469
Teacher	18,105–33,150
Inner London teacher	21,522–39,093
Police	£
Superintendent	49,077–57,249
Sergeant	29,307–32,940
Constable	18,666–29,307
Army (on appointment)	£
Lieutenant-Colonel	54,932
Major	39,140

Captain	31,069
Lieutenant	24,247

National Health Service	£
Enrolled nurse	13,465–16,525
Staff nurse	16,525–18,240
Senior staff nurse	17,660–21,325
Ward sister	19,585–25,360
Senior ward sister	23,110–33,820
Consultant	54,340–70,715
Cabinet minister	71,433

How children spend their money

In 2000/1 children aged 7–15 spent:
- £12.30 per week on average.
- Girls spent more than boys, £13.20 per week compared with £11.20.
- Girls were more likely than boys to spend their money on clothing and footwear, and on personal goods such as toiletries and cosmetics.
- Boys were more likely than girls to spend their money on food and non-alcoholic drink, and on leisure goods such as computer games, CDs and videos.

Office for National Statistics (2002)

Parental spending

The average parent spends nearly £133 on each child to prepare for the new school year.

Survey by Capital One, 2004

Greater reported occupational stress is associated with the following factors. To compare your stress levels award yourself a point for each of the following.

If you are …
- middle-aged
- widowed/divorced or separated
- educated to degree level
- in full-time employment earning over £20,000
- in an occupation such as teaching, nursing or being a manager (or being in social group II).

'Occupational stress is perceived as a major problem by teachers, nurses and managers.'

Smith (2000)

Stress points

In 2000 a Health and Safety Executive report put teachers at the top of the stress league table. Based on a survey of 17,000 people it found:

Teachers reporting high stress:	41.5 per cent.
Nurses reporting high stress:	31.8 per cent.
Managers reporting high stress:	27.8 per cent.

Stressed workers are 25 per cent more likely to suffer a heart attack and 50 per cent more prone to fatal strokes.

Reported in The Times Educational Supplement, *19 March 2004*

Excessive workload

The following activities were agreed by the DfES and teacher unions as 'common tasks' that 'need not routinely be carried out by teachers and should be that to support staff'.

Test yourself. Score 1 mark if you have never done such a task, 2 marks if you no longer do so, minus 1 if you still do:

- collecting money
- collating pupil reports
- stocktaking
- chasing absences
- administering work experience
- cataloguing, preparing, issuing and maintaining equipment and materials
- bulk photocopying
- administering examinations
- minuting meetings
- copy typing
- invigilating examinations
- coordinating and submitting bids
- producing class lists
- administering teacher cover
- seeking and giving personnel advice
- record keeping and filing
- ICT troubleshooting and minor repairs
- managing pupil data
- classroom display
- commissioning new ICT equipment
- inputting pupil data
- analysing attendance figures
- ordering supplies and equipment
- processing exam results
- producing standard letters.

Why teachers leave teaching

Turnover (loss from schools)	14.1 per cent (2002)
Wastage (loss from the maintained sector)	7.9 per cent (2002)

Five main reasons for teachers leaving teaching:
- workload (most important)
- new challenge
- the school situation (includes poor pupil behaviour)
- personal circumstances
- salary.

Where do the teachers go?

Of every 100 teachers resigning:
- 40 moved to other maintained schools
- 13 retired (9 prematurely)
- 9 went on maternity leave or to care for family members
- 7 moved to supply teaching
- 7 went to other teaching posts (independent schools, FE and HE)
- 5 continued in 'other employment'
- 4 took up 'other education posts'
- 4 left to to travel
- 11 went to destinations unknown.

Spot the likely leavers

Leavers tended to be:
either young with a few years' service;
or older and approaching retirement;
female;
from the shortage subjects.

Teachers in London and the south and east were more likely to move to other schools and to leave than teachers in the midlands and the north.

Any chance of your coming back?

The main changes that would have made a difference to the others were:
a reduced workload
more support from the school
a higher salary.

The percentage of leavers who said that nothing would have induced them to stay: > 40 per cent.

Would you return to teaching?

Number of leavers who thought it 'very likely' that they would return to teaching full time: 13 per cent.

Number who would consider part-time work: < 13 per cent.
Number who were contemplating supply: 25 per cent.
Number who, after one or two terms, were sure they had done
   the right thing: 98 per cent.
Number who had started teaching again, usually part time:
   10 per cent.
                                        Smithers and Robinson (2000b)

Workforce reform

Only improved pupil behaviour will make life easier for teachers. What
is to blame for the sharp decline in pupil behaviour?
- the overloaded curriculum for 11–14-year-olds.
- parental attitudes
- large class sizes
- inclusion strategies
- lack of time for pupils and teachers to talk to each other due to
  pastoral and administrative responsibilities.
                                        Smithers and Robinson (2000a)

The five biggest documents sent to schools in 2003

1. *Teachers Pay and Conditions* (DfES) – 180 pages
2. *Key Stage 3 National Strategy, Year 9 booster kit – English*
   (DfES) – 170 pages
3. *KS3 targeting level 5 and above – teaching responses to reading*
   (DfES) – 122 pages
4. *Annual Report of Her Majesty's Chief Inspector of Schools
   2001–2* (Ofsted) – 106 pages
5. *Handbook for Inspectors – Inspector of Connexions
   partnerships* (Ofsted) – 89 pages

Long service

It is reported that the longest teaching career was of more than 80 years,
a record held by Medarda de Jesus Leonde Uzcategui of Venezuela
who taught in Caracas, Venezuela starting in 1911.

Epitaph

The last bell has rung
The last lesson is over
The classroom is empty and I sag.
Young shouting echoes and trickles away
Silence falls like chalk dust into a pale stillness.
Peace.
I can relax
My teaching is done and I have learned my last lesson.
I feel lighter. I am not empty
But 30 years of grim schoolmaster
Have slipped from my shoulders.
The English teacher's sentence is finished.

Author

Teacher sickness absence 2002

Average teacher days off sick: 5.3
Of those who took sickness absence, on average,
    9.3 days were taken per teacher.
Number of staff off sick: 293,200
Percentage of staff off sick: 57 per cent
Total days taken as sickness absence: 2,741,600
Cost to the UK economy of teacher absenteeism: approximately
    £368 million every year.

Pupil absence

Maintained primary schools
- Authorized absences: 5.39 per cent.
- Unauthorized absences: 0.43 per cent.
- Total absences: 5.82 per cent.

Maintained secondary schools
- Authorized absences: 7.21 per cent.
- Unauthorized absences: 1.08 per cent.
- Total absences: 8.29 per cent.

DfES 2002/3 provisional figures

Student depression

Number of prescriptions for anti-depressants given to students in full-time education:

16–18-year-olds: 140,000 (2003) – up from 46,000 in 1995
under-16: 110,000 (2003) – up from 76,000 in 1996.

Medicines and Healthcare Products Regulatory Agency (MHRA)

School time

Children spend 85 per cent of their waking hours outside school.

Parliamentary absence

On 20 January 2004 the House of Commons held a debate on truancy in schools.

They concluded that while attendance and behaviour were 'central' to raising school standards, there was no 'magic wand' to compel full attendance.

Of the country's 659 MPs the attendance varied from 12 to 20 in a four-hour debate.

Truancy

The number of secondary school pupils missing at least one half-day a year has jumped by almost 40 per cent in the six years since Labour came to power.

In the same period, spending to improve classroom behaviour has risen by 700 per cent.

The Financial Times, *6 January 2004*

Arson

Average number of arson attacks per week on schools
in the UK: 16

Proportion of schools suffering a fire: 1 in 15

Percentage of all school fires that are caused by arson: 75 per cent.

DfES

The number of schools damaged or destroyed by fire has risen by 170
per cent (1993–2003):

Average no. of schools per week catching fire: 20

Percentage of fires caused by pupils: 90

Proportion of offenders aged 10–14:   66 per cent

No. of pupils whose education is disrupted: 100,000

Area most at risk: Greater Manchester and West
                        Yorkshire, where at least one school
                        is seriously damaged each week

The cost rose from £27.1 million in 1993 to £73.4 million in 2003.

No. of schools fitted with sprinkler systems: 150 of 28,000.

http://www.arsonpreventionbureau.org.uk/

Exclusions

In 1996/7 permanent exclusions from maintained schools peaked at
12,700, three times the figure for the early and mid-1990s.

Permanent exclusions in 2001/2: 9,535 – up 400 from 2000/1.

Nearly two-thirds of young offenders of school age who are sentenced
in court have been excluded from school or truant significantly.

In 2001/2 the rate of exclusion of black Caribbean pupils was three
times that for white pupils. Indian and Chinese ethnic groups have the
lowest rates of exclusion.

The lowest exclusion rates are in primary schools, where 3 in every
10,000 pupils are excluded. This rate has remained constant over the last
five years.

DfES (2003a)

Permanent exclusions

Number of permanent exclusions in the year 2002–3: 9,535 (just 0.12 per cent of the whole school population).

Of these, 7,741 (0.24 per cent of the total population) were from the secondary sector.

Of these exclusions 82 per cent were of boys, most commonly at 13 or 14 years old (24.7 and 26.7 per cent respectively).

DfES (2003a)

Attacks

NAS/UWT members recorded 964 incidents of physical and verbal abuse in one ten-day period, including 126 physical attacks.

School killings

Killings in US schools tripled in 2004 to 48, the highest in a decade. Critics blamed this on budget cuts of $28 million in safety and drug programmes in schools. Guns or knives were involved in most of the deaths.

(The figures include all violent non-natural deaths at school, at a school event or on the way to or from school.)

In April 1999 2 teenagers shot dead 12 students and a teacher at Columbine High School in Littleton, Colorado before killing themselves.

The Times, *29 June 2004*

On 4 November 2003 Luke Walmsley, 14, was fatally stabbed by a 15-year-old in the corridor at Birkbeck Secondary School in North Somercotes, Lincolnshire.

The Times, *9 July 2004*

Reasons for vandalism

- The excitement involved in avoiding detection
- The pleasure experienced when destroying property
- The relief provided from frustration or anger.

From Brog and Voltenauer-Lagemann (1989)

'Boredom'
'Fun'
It's a laugh ...'

Boys on the street corner

Lack of things to do
Existing disorder in the area
Unemployment
Peer pressure.

Pollard (1988) cited in Coffield (1991). Quoted in 'Crime Reduction Toolkits': http://www.crimereduction.gov.uk/toolkits

- Landscape designs such as mounds or bridges may make missile attacks easier and more tempting.
- Existing damage or graffiti may prompt or encourage further acts.
- The appearance of sterile environments may tempt vandals.
- Envy of those with more possessions may lead to anti-authoritarian acts including theft and criminal damage.

Security in schools

Consider:
- Deterrence, Detection and Detention
- CCTV to monitor access points and vulnerable locations
- Fire detection devices and automatic sprinklers or gaseous extinguishing systems
- Visitor identification systems and ID cards
- Secure locks throughout premises
- Push-button locks on internal doors
- Panic alarms – either fixed or portable.

Security Dos and Don'ts for schools

Do buy the best system you can afford – cut price security is no security.

Do deal with basic security issues first – keep valuables out of sight, close windows, lock drawers and cabinets, approach strangers on the site.

Do make sure all staff know how to evacuate the buildings.

Don't regard security as a cost – it can reduce both loss and insurance premiums.

Don't destroy the learning environment by making the school a fortress.

Don't rely only on an alarm – it's just a prompt to tell you to respond.

Don't assume it only happens to someone else.

Safety in schools

Accidents will happen, but the following may reduce the chance of an accident while children are in your care:

- Check continually for broken or damaged chairs and desks, door handles, carpets.
- Check windows at least daily. Latches should be firm, no cracks in glass, glass secure in the frame. Open and close them yourself or at least make sure you watch while older children do so.
- Make written requests for repairs and follow up your requests if they are not completed promptly.
- Supervise entry, exit and movement around the room.
- Make sure pupils' bags are tidied away during lessons.
- Check all leads and wiring are safe before use. Don't tuck wires tidily between door and door jamb where they could be nipped or cut. Don't use cracked sockets or plugs.
- As an integral part of an ICT lesson enforce good posture (forearms horizontal, back quite straight, eyes not too close to the screen).

According to the Child Accident Prevention Trust

Number of children aged 5–11 visiting hospital accident and emergency departments in 1999 as a result of accidents at schools: > 160,000.

Of these …

Number attending A&E after having been 'bumped into': > 80,000.

Number attending as a result of 'pinching, crushing, cutting, tearing or puncturing themselves': > 9,000.

Falls account for the largest number of children's accidents both in the home and outside.

Road accidents cause the largest number of serious injuries and deaths.

Number of children hurt in road accidents on Britain's roads every year: 40,000.

Of these …

Children killed: approximately 200.

Children seriously injured: a further 5,000.

Proportion of all deaths of children and young people aged 5–19 due to road accidents in 2000: 20 per cent.

Reduction in numbers of childhood deaths between 1980 and 2001: 100 per cent.

Childhood deaths for age 1–14 in 1980: 2,971.

Childhood deaths for age 1–14 in 2001: 1,420.

Childhood deaths for age 10–14 in 1980: 919.

Childhood deaths for age 10–14 in 2001: 459.

The Child Accident Prevention Trust

School trips stopped by sunshine

Derby City Council advised head teachers to consider cancelling school trips and sports days if the weather is too sunny. The risk of skin cancer is too great, it believes.

The Council also advises that teachers use spray-on sunscreen – to avoid making physical contact with children by rubbing it into their skin.

Meanwhile a Professor of Medicine at Boston University has identified an 'unrecognized epidemic' of vitamin D deficiency that is itself causing deaths from other cancers, and rickets because so many people are wearing sunblock.

He advocates five to ten minutes of unprotected sun exposure to the face, arms and hands between 10am and 3pm two to three times a week, then covering up with sunscreen, hats and clothes.

Road deaths among children

Average number of children killed on the roads (early 1980s): approximately 560 deaths per year.

Average number of children killed on the roads (1990): 221.

Average number of children killed on the roads (2000): 191.

Most children killed or seriously injured are pedestrians rather than car passengers or cyclists.

Children's risk of being involved in a traffic accident increases as they grow older, with a marked increase in accident rates among 10–13-year-olds.

Office for National Statstics (2002)

How do children travel to school?

Children aged 5–10 walking to school: 56 per cent.
Children aged 11–16 walking to school: 43 per cent.

Primary school children travelling by car to school: 36 per cent.
Secondary school children travelling by car to school: 19 per cent.

Primary school children travelling by bus to school: 7 per cent.
Secondary school children travelling by bus to school: 32 per cent.

Average distance from home to secondary school: 3 miles.
Average distance from home to primary school: 1.5 miles.

Department for Transport (1998–2000)

Home discipline

When I was younger, if a pupil was in trouble with their teacher, they were in trouble with their parents too. It is not always the case today, but it should be.

Tony Blair, addressing head teachers in Cardiff, May 2004

School policy

- Schools should have a clear vision for managing behaviour.
- Establish clear rules and boundaries.
- Emphasize the positive – 'good behaviour' rather than 'discipline'.
- Teachers should model behaviour and interactions in a positive and supportive way.
- Establish clear boundaries and known sanctions.
- Emphasize praise and reward good behaviour.
- Make a clear distinction between appropriate and inappropriate behaviour.
- Be clear on which behaviour is totally unacceptable.

The quality of teaching and learning has a significant impact on pupils' behaviour.

From Teachernet: http://www.teachernet.gov.uk/supplyteachers/

Homophobia

Being fat is the most common cause of bullying.
Being thought of as gay is second.

Homosexual adolescents are two to three times more likely to commit suicide or harm themselves than heterosexual adolescents.

School-age pupils who are homosexual:
approximately 10 per cent.
School-age pupils who had experienced some form of
homosexual activity: > 1 per cent boys, 5 per cent girls.

Schools claiming to be aware of homophobic bullying:
80 per cent.
Schools having a policy addressing homophobic bullying:
6 per cent.

The Times Educational Supplement, 28 May 2003

Pie face

A student who won a charity contest to throw a pie in his principal's face was expelled when he threw it too hard. Police said, 'It wasn't just a toss. He smashed the pie in her face.'

Parental responsibility

Parents must now be held responsible for the indiscipline of their offspring. It is time that society realized that it is the role of the teacher to teach. It is not the role of a teacher to be a surrogate parent or a social worker or, heaven help us, a policeman.

Nicholas Griffin, leader of the Professional Association of Teachers

Crimes committed by children

The proportion of offenders peaks at 18 years old for boys and 15 for girls and then declines.
16-year-old boys in England and Wales found guilty of, or cautioned for, indictable offences in 2000: 6 per cent.
16-year-old girls in England and Wales found guilty of, or cautioned for, indictable offences in 2000: 1.5 per cent.

Office for National Statistics (2002)

Type of offence

Most common offence for both boys and girls (2000): theft and handling stolen goods.
Number of 15-year-olds cautioned or found guilty of theft and handling stolen goods: > 11,000.
Number of 10-year-olds cautioned or found guilty of theft and handling stolen goods: < 1,000.

Office for National Statistics (2002)

How Pippa became senior man in the Junior Common Room

Punishment at Eton

Beating was just part of life. You were summoned ceremonially to the Library by the senior boys of the house after evening prayers. I was deemed to be a sort of subversive influence and the House Captain decided that although I had not flouted any particular law I had accumulated sufficient small omissions or sins to warrant a beating. It was extremely painful – a genuine, old-fashioned beating which drew blood.

The Eton birches were intimidating instruments consisting of three feet of handle and two of a thick bunch of birch twigs. A dozen new rods were supposed to be at hand every morning since there was no calculating the number of floggings which might be inflicted in a day.

A boy 'complained of' by a master or tutor, for any one of a long list of possible offences and also for idleness at lessons, would be 'put in the bill' (the flogging list). Then, at the appointed hour, he would be birched by either the Head or the Lower Master, depending on his position in the school. In the Lower School the 'executions' were always fully public and the boys would gather to watch the fun, with Upper School boys also permitted to attend.

Accounts of Eton beatings at http://home.freeuk.net/mkb/pubschool.htm

Thomas Arnold's views on flogging

I have so far got rid of the birch that I only flogged seven boys last half year and the same number hitherto in this. I never did nor do I believe that it can be relinquished altogether – but I think it may well be reserved for offences either great in themselves or rendered great by frequent repetition; and then it should be administered in earnest.

Quoted in Thomas Arnold, Headmaster *by Michael McCrum (1989)*

A cut above the rest

A 40-year-old male teacher in Fukuoka City, Japan forced a pupil to write an apology in his own blood for dozing off in his lesson. The teacher, who handed the boy a blade and forced him to cut himself, has expressed remorse.

The Times, 22 June 2004

Attempts to outwit Ofsted

1. *Change teachers* 'Endeavour High' school in Hull drafted in experienced teachers from other schools to help it through its Ofsted inspection.
2. *Move out pupils* 'Endeavour High' also arranged for its most disruptive students to be away on a course at a local college during the inspection.

   An Ofsted spokesman said the action of the school 'did not appear to be illegal'.
3. *Fake illness* 'OFSTED FEAR TEACHER WHO FAKED LEUKAEMIA IS BANNED'

   A primary school teacher who was so frightened of undergoing Ofsted inspection that she pretended to be suffering from leukaemia was banned from teaching for four years. She took time off to attend fictitious hospital appointments and would sit in her classroom touching her stomach, claiming to be in agony.

   Eventually another head teacher revealed that she had used the same scam at a previous school before an inspection. She explained, 'It was absolute fear of an inspection from Ofsted. Not because I was a bad or failing teacher, but because I was so frightened of the inspection due to my own lack of confidence.'

   PA News, 29 March 2004

Drugs

11–15-year-olds who had taken illegal drugs in the previous year: 20 per cent.

Most commonly used illegal drug: cannabis – taken by 13 per cent of those surveyed.

Social Focus in Brief: Children (2002), in: www.statistics.gov.uk/statbase

Over-performing does not convince an Ofsted inspector

Misbehaviour in class is not a recent problem

Alcohol

11–15-year-olds reporting that they had ever drunk alcohol (2001): 60 per cent.

11–15-year-olds reporting that they had drunk alcohol in the last week (2001): 25 per cent.

Of those who had drunk alcohol (1990), the average number of units drunk in the previous week: boys 5.7, girls 4.7.

Of those who had drunk alcohol (2001), the average number of units drunk in the previous week: boys 10.6, girls 8.9.

Office for National Statistics (2002)

Our revels now are ended

Traditionally, Oxford University students have celebrated the end of their finals in June with boisterous behaviour. Examples include: throwing flour bombs, spraying champagne, jumping into the River Cherwell – either in dinner jackets or entirely naked.

However, recently behaviour has got out of hand. Examples include emptying buckets of pigs' offal over fellow students, 'fluid-spraying and egg-hurling'.

Now the university will impose £70 fines for bad public behaviour. Fines start at £30 for spraying fizzy wine and go up to £70 for firing high-velocity water pistols.

The only legally throwable items are glitter or confetti.

'It is just another example of the university trying to control every aspect of students' lives,' said a student.

The Guardian, *23 April 2004*

Schoolgirls' top ten role models (April 2004)

1.	Dawn French	6.	Dame Judi Dench
2.	J.K. Rowling	7.	Paula Radcliffe
3.	The Calendar Girls	8.	Kerry McFadden
4.	Lisa Potts	9.	Ms Dynamite
5.	Dido	10.	Kate Winslet

How many education secretaries do you remember?

Asked to name the current Education Secretary:

Teachers unable to do so: 53 per cent.

Teachers under the age of 30 unable to do so: 80 per cent.

Most common reply: 'I don't know'.

Teachers suggesting alternative names: 6 per cent.

December 2003

Answer at the time (look away now
if you don't want to see): Charles Clarke

Secretaries of State for Education

1970	Margaret Thatcher
1979–81	Mark Carlisle
1981–6	Keith Joseph
1986–9	Kenneth Baker
1989–90	John MacGregor
1990–2	Kenneth Clarke
1992–4	John Patten
1994–7	Gillian Shepherd
1997–2001	David Blunkett
2001–2	Estelle Morris
2002–4	Charles Clarke
2004–	Ruth Kelly

Great educationalists –
how many do you know about?

Matthew Arnold (1822–88)
An inspector's:

> first duty is to verify the conditions on which public aid is offered to schools and to assure the department that the nation is obtaining its outlay. But he is called upon to visit schools of very different types, to observe carefully the merits and demerits of each, to recognise very varied forms of good work, to place himself in sympathy with teachers and their difficulties, convey suggestions as to methods he has observed elsewhere, and to leave behind him at every school some stimulus to improvement.

Fitch (1897)

John Dewey (1859–1952)
He has been described as having given the most significant contribution to the development of educational thinking in the twentieth century. He believed that education must engage with and enlarge experience, especially a democratic and social experience. His exploration of thinking and reflection – and the role of educators in this – has influenced a great deal of education in the USA and the UK.

> I believe that under existing conditions far too much of the stimulus and control proceeds from the teacher, because of neglect of the idea of the school as a form of social life.

Dewey (1897)

Friedrich Wilhelm August Froebel (1782–1852)
Started as a worker in the forest at Turingen. Later worked as an assistant school teacher under Pestalozzi. Convinced that natural science was the basis for the best education, his kindergarten and primary schools provided organized and well-directed play as a means of acquiring knowledge and understanding.

Maria Montessori (1870–1952)
Physician and educationist, born in Rome. She was the first woman in Italy to graduate in medicine. Later she joined the psychiatric clinic, and

became interested in the problems of mentally handicapped children. She opened her first 'children's house' in 1907, developing a system of education for children aged three to six, based on freedom of movement, the provision of considerable choice for pupils, and the use of specially designed activities and equipment.

Henry Morris (1889–1961)
Secretary for Education in Cambridgeshire who championed rural education and lifelong learning and developed the Village College system, of which Sawston Village College (1930) was the first.

A(lexander) S(utherland) Neill (1883–1973)
Educationist and writer, born in Kingsmuir, Fife, E Scotland, UK. He studied at Edinburgh and taught in many different schools. He started a community school near Salzburg, which developed into Summerhill School in Leiston, Suffolk (1927). It was an experimental co-educational progressive school. Neill spent a lot of time using psychotherapy to understand the many difficult children at the school. He was the most radical of British progressive schoolteachers.

Johann Heinrich Pestalozzi (1746–1827)
Educationist, and pioneer of mass education for poor children, born in Zürich, N Switzerland. He worked as a farmer and later opened a school at Berthoud (Burgdorf), where he wrote 'How Gertrude Educates her Children' in 1801. This is the standard work on the Pestalozzian method. The process of education is seen as a gradual unfolding, prompted by observation, of the children's innate facilities. Pestalozzi International Children's Villages have been established at Trogen, Switzerland (1946) and Sedlescombe, Surrey, UK (1958).

Jean-Jacques Rousseau (1712–78)
Philosopher, author, political theorist and composer. Born 28 June 1712, in Geneva, Switzerland. One of the greatest figures of the French Enlightenment. His philosophy of education is expressed in *Emile* (1762), based on natural development and the power of example.

Rudolph Steiner (1861–1925)
Social philosopher, the founder of anthroposophy, born in Kraljevec, NW Croatia. He studied science and mathematics, and edited Goethe's scientific papers. In 1912 he established his first 'school of spiritual science', in Switzerland. His aim was to integrate the psychological and practical dimensions of life into an educational, ecological and therapeutic basis for spiritual and physical development. Rudolf Steiner Schools focus on the development of the whole personality of the child.

William Waynflete (Bishop of Winchester 1447–86)
Waynflete was one of the great educationalists and patrons of learning of late medieval England. He played a leading role in some of the changes that transformed education in fifteenth-century England: college development in Oxford and Cambridge; humanist ideas; the teaching of Greek; new grammars; and the introduction of printing as a means of disseminating the new learning.

Fifty major thinkers on education – how many have you heard of?

Confucius	551–479 BC
Socrates	469–399 BC
Plato	427–347 BC
Aristotle	384–322 BC
Jesus	AD 4–29
St Augustine	354–430
Al-Ghazzali	1058–1111
Ibn Tufayl	1106–85
Desiderius Erasmus	1466–1536
Jan Amos Comenius	1592–1670
John Locke	1632–1704
John Wesley	1703–91
Jean-Jacques Rousseau	1712–78
Immanuel Kant	1724–1804
Johann Heinrich Pestalozzi	1746–1827
Mary Wollstonecraft	1759–97
John Gottlieb Fichte	1762–1814
Wilhelm von Humboldt	1767–1835

Georg Wilhelm Friedrich Hegel	1770–1831
Johann Friedrich Herbart	1776–1841
Friedrich Wilhelm August Froebel	1782–1852
John Henry Newman	1801–90
John Stuart Mill	1806–73
Charles Darwin	1809–82
John Ruskin	1819–1900
Herbert Spencer	1820–1903
Matthew Arnold	1822–88
Thomas Henry Huxley	1825–95
Louisa May Alcott	1832–88
Samuel Butler	1835–1902
Robert Morant	1836–1920
Eugenio Maria de Hostos	1839–1903
Friedrich Nietzsche	1844–1900
Alfred Binet	1857–1911
Emile Durkheim	1858–1917
Anna Julia Haywood Cooper	1858–1964
John Dewey	1859–1952
Jane Addams	1860–1935
Rudolf Steiner	1861–1925
Rabindranath Tagore	1861–1941
Alfred North Whitehead	1861–1947
Emile Jaques-Dalcroze	1865–1950
William Edward Burghard Du Bois	1868–1963
M.K. Gandhi	1869–1948
Maria Montessori	1870–1952
Bertrand Russell	1872–1970
E.L. Thorndike	1874–1949
Martin Buber	1878–1965
José Ortega y Gasset	1883–1955
Cyril Lodovic Burt	1883–1971

From Palmer (ed.) (2001)

How many pupils?

There are 8.4 million pupils in 25,500 maintained and independent schools in England.

Pupils taught in maintained nursery, primary
and secondary schools: 92 per cent.
Pupils attending independent schools: 7 per cent.
Pupils attending maintained and
non-maintained special schools: 1 per cent.

DfES (2003a)

Staying at home

It is estimated that 'up to 170,000 children' are being taught by their parents in England and Wales.

The Times, *30 July 2004*

How many pupils per teacher in England?

In maintained nursery, primary and secondary schools: 17.9 pupils.
In independent schools: 9.7 pupils.

DfES (2003a)

Pupil:staff ratio at Millfield School: 1:7.5.
More than 130 staff take part in the games programme.

PE&Sport Today, *Summer 2004*

Getting larger or smaller?

Change in pupil:teacher ratio in primary schools 1983–2003:
up from 22.3 to 22.6.
Change in pupil:teacher ratio in secondary schools 1983–2003:
up from 16.5 to 17.

Change in pupil:teacher ratio in independent schools 1983–2003: down from 11.9 to 9.7 (8.8 in the south east).

DfES (2003a)

Independent school numbers

Number of pupils in independent schools:

UK	620,000
England	571,000
Wales	9,500
Scotland	32,300
Northern Ireland	7,400

School size (January 2003)

Most maintained primary schools:	100–300 pupils
Fewer than 100 pupils:	2,702 schools
800–900 pupils:	7 schools.
Most maintained secondary schools:	600–1,200 pupils
Fewer than 100 pupils:	2 schools
Over 1,800 pupils:	63 schools.
Most independent schools:	50–300 pupils
Largest single inner London independent school:	3,605 pupils
Fewer than 25 pupils:	199 schools.

DfES (2003a)

Largest school

The Guinness Book of Records gives the largest school (as judged by pupil numbers) as the City Montessori School, Lucknow, India, with 26,312 on the roll.

You think you've got a large class?

(Classes with a single teacher)

Maintained primary schools: 149,207 classes (average class size: 26.3).
Of these, classes of 41 or more pupils: 140.
Most of these (34) were in the north west.

Classes of 31–35 pupils: 23.7 per cent (1999) to 12.1 per cent (2003).
Number of Key Stage 1 pupils in classes of 31 or more taught by
one teacher (January 2003): 16,400.

In secondary schools, of 52,417 classes taught by a single teacher, 31 had
41 or more pupils. Of these large classes 13 were in Year 12.
Average class size: 21.9.

DfES (2003a)

Largest simultaneous lesson

The world's largest simultaneous lesson was held as part of Learning
Day by Birmingham City Council on 21 March 2002. There were
28,101 pupils learning a phrase in a variety of languages.

Pupils in mainstream schools, England, 1970–2002 (actual) and 2003–5 (projected)

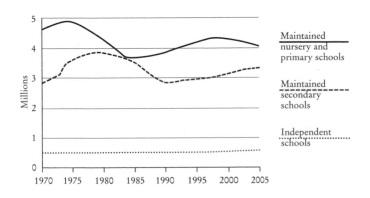

- The 25 per cent fall in the number of maintained nursery and
  primary school pupils between 1974 and 1985 can be explained
  by a 35 per cent fall in the number of births between 1964 and
  1977. The number of secondary school pupils fell by 26 per
  cent between 1979 and 1991.
- After increasing throughout the 1990s, the total number of
  nursery and primary school pupils peaked in 1998 and the fall

since then is projected to continue. By 2005, the total will have reverted back to about its 1993 level.
- The number of secondary school pupils is expected to peak at 3.33 million in 2004.

DfES Trends in Education and Skills

Net enrolment ratios in Africa

Primary education

Sub-Saharan Africa:	60 per cent (1998)

(In other words, four children out of ten of primary-school age were not enrolled at a school.)

Central and Western Africa:	54 per cent
Eastern and Southern Africa:	67 per cent

Secondary education:

Central and Western Africa:	18 per cent
Eastern and Southern Africa:	29 per cent
Botswana:	77 per cent
Mozambique:	9 per cent

(So in Mozambique, on average, fewer than one in ten children aged 11–16 attend school.)

UNESCO (2001)

Pupil:teacher ratio in primary education in Africa

Average number of pupils per teacher:	40
Number of countries with a pupil:teacher ratio below 32:1:	10
Number of countries with a pupil:teacher ratio of over 50:1:	10

Uganda	60:1
Mali and Congo	> 60:1
Mozambique	61:1
Chad	68:1

African illiteracy and pupil:teacher ratios

Country	Illiteracy rates at 15yrs in %		Pupil:teacher ratio in primary education in %	Net intake rate at primary school in %	
	M	F		School age	Age +1
Botswana	27	22	28	–	–
Burkina Faso	68	87	49	19	12
Ethiopia	58	70	–	22	18
Gambia	58	73	33	10	45
Guinea-Bissau	43	83	35	33	19
Mozambique	42	73	61	12	27
Niger	78	93	41	26	6
Senegal	55	74	49	39	16
South Africa	15	16	–	–	–
Zimbabwe	8	17	41	40	42

UNESCO (2001)

Universal primary education

It is estimated that, at the current rate of funding, universal primary education in sub-Saharan Africa will not be achieved until the year 2129.

Traditional literacy

Percentage of miners in Northumberland and Durham in 1840 who could read: 79.

Percentage of adults in Hull who were literate in 1841: 92.

Percentage of the working class who were literate in the 1830s: estimated between two-thirds and three-quarters.

It is probable that at some point between 1880 and 1939 the UK was very near to a state of universal literacy.

Quoted in Boyson (1975)

'Life at 33'

Of a representative cohort of 11,633 people:
- 12 per cent acknowledged some difficulty with literacy or numeracy
- 4 per cent said they had a literacy problem
- 10 per cent said they had a writing or spelling problem
- 3 per cent said they had a numeracy problem.

Of those reporting a literacy problem, spelling was a difficulty for 93 per cent of men and 96 per cent of women.

Of those reporting a numeracy problem, multiplying and dividing were reported as difficult by about three-quarters of the group.

Ferri (1993)

The school library

What a school thinks about its library is a measure of what it thinks about education.

Harold Howe, former US Commissioner of Education

Language

The first language of 10.5 per cent of primary school pupils and 8.8 per cent of secondary school pupils was known or believed to be other than English.

DfES (2003a)

Reading for enjoyment or for literacy?

An NFER poll of 5,000 children aged 9 and 11 showed that the percentage of the older children enjoying stories had fallen from 77 to 65. Pollsters suggested that the fall might be linked to the rigidity of the National Literacy Strategy.

The children surveyed were the first to have received five years of teaching according to the National Literacy Strategy – all of their school careers in the case of the 9-year-olds.

Of boys aged 11, 55 per cent enjoyed reading stories – 15 percentage points fewer than five years previously.

Modern literacy

Children reaching the expected level in English:
Government target: 80 per cent.
Percentage achieved in 1997: 63 per cent.
Percentage achieved in 2002: 75 per cent.

The National Literacy Strategy was introduced in 1998.

Ontario Institute for Studies in Education (2003)

If, as many suspect, children are not being taught to read and write properly under the Government's prescriptive lesson plans, it will be the biggest imposition of poor teaching methods in the history of English education.

'Difficult decisions are looming for Clarke', Liz Lightfoot, the Daily Telegraph, *25 October 2002*

Famous dyslexics

Nelson Rockefeller	Fred Astaire
Cher	Susan Hampshire
Gustave Flaubert	Michelangelo
Sir Winston Churchill	Duncan Goodhew
Thomas Edison	Steven Spielberg
W.B. Yeats	King Carl Gustav XVI of Sweden
Agatha Christie	Charles Darwin
Albert Einstein	Sir Isaac Newton
Tom Cruise	Benjamin Zephaniah
Leonardo Da Vinci	David Bailey
General George Patton	Marlon Brando
Richard Branson	Noel Gallagher
Michael Heseltine	Felicity Kendall
Sir Anthony Hopkins	Nicholas Negroponte
Tommy Hilfiger	Sir Stephen Redgrave

http://www.garry.karen.btinternet.co.uk/famous.dyslexics.htm
http://maher.maddsites.com/dyslexia/

Owed to autumn

- Keats made four spelling mistakes in the first ten lines of 'Ode to Autumn'.
- US President Andrew Jackson said, 'It is a damn poor mind that can only think of one way to spell a word.'

Cook (2004)

US children 'hooked on television at two'

Percentage of two-year-old children spending an average of 125 minutes per day watching TV or a computer screen: 68.

Percentage of children under two watching TV every day: 52.

Percentage of children under two watching videos or DVDs every day: 42.

Percentage of US families with no rules restricting the length of time their children watched TV: 21.

Percentage of parents of four- to six-year-old boys who had seen their sons imitating aggressive behaviour on television: 65.

Percentage of US children under six with a television by their bed: 34.

Percentage of US children under three who have used a computer without help: 27.

Percentage of US children under six who live in homes where the television is on at least half the time: 66.

Percentage of US children under six who live in a household without a television: 1.

Study by the Henry J. Kaiser Family Foundation,
reported in The Times, *30 October 2003*

The headmaster's new policy had been largely misunderstood, reflected Thribling

Pupils' first language

Having a first language other than English:

- in maintained primary schools in England:
  Overall   10.5 per cent (365,000)
  West Midlands   12.9 per cent
  Inner London   49.4 per cent
- in secondary maintained schools in England:
  Overall   8.8 per cent (292,360)
  Inner London   45.6 per cent

DfES (2003a)

Languages spoken in London schools

It is estimated that some 300 languages are regularly spoken within the capital.

Ten most common mother tongues for children in London

Language	Approximate total
English	608,500
Bengali and Silheti	40,400
Punjabi	29,800
Gujerati	28,699
Hindi/Urdu	26,000
Turkish	15,600
Arabic	11,000
English-based Creoles	10,700
Yoruba	10,400
Somali	8,300

Evening Standard, *21 January 2000*

In maintained nursery and primary schools in England:
    Total roll: 4,350,260
    Took free school meals: 604,911 (13.9 per cent)
    Known to be eligible: 16.8 per cent.

So 2.9 per cent would not eat them even if they were free.

	Took free school meals (%)	Eligible (%)
Inner London	31.3	37.2
North East	19.1	22.1
South East	7.9	10.1

In maintained secondary schools in England:
    Total roll: 3,308,492
    Took free school meals: 349,777 (10.6 per cent)
    Known to be eligible: 14.5 per cent.

	Took free school meals (%)	Eligible (%)
Inner London	31	39.4
North West	13.9	18.8
South East	6	8.4

DfES (2003a)

Free milk

The School Milk Act of 1946 provided a free third of a pint of milk to all schoolchildren. This remained until 1970 when it was withdrawn from secondary school pupils by Margaret Thatcher as education minister, earning her the name 'Milk Snatcher'.

School dinners

Margaret Thatcher raised the charge for school meals to 12p in April 1971 and to 14p in April 1973.

Having been withdrawn in the 1970s, statutory nutritional guidelines were restored in 2001. Schools are required to offer fruit, vegetables, meat or fish, carbohydrates and dairy products. Red meat should be served three times per week and fish twice.

Surveys show that, given a free choice, many pupils prefer crisps, chips, chocolate and sugary soft drinks.

A self-monitoring lunch checklist

Compulsory requirements

(Primary age. Other ages vary slightly.) Is at least one item from each of the following food groups present on the daily menu and throughout the lunch service?

Bread, other cereals and potatoes (must not be cooked in fat or oil on more than three days a week)	Yes/No
Vegetables and salads	Yes/No
Fruit and fruit juice (Are fruit-based desserts available at least twice a week?)	Yes/No
Milk and dairy foods (Are lower-fat alternatives provided?)	Yes/No
Meat, fish and alternative sources of protein	Yes/No
Is red meat available at least two times a week? (Which types of red meat are served?)	Yes/No
Is fish available at least once a week? (Is oily fish served and if so how often?)	Yes/No
Strong recommendation Is drinking water available free of charge every day?	Yes/No
Does the menu cycle feature each week: foods rich in iron?	Yes/No
foods rich in calcium?	Yes/No
a variety of fresh fruit and vegetables?	Yes/No
foods rich in zinc?	Yes/No

> *Have healthy catering practices been adopted, for example:*
> Are alternatives to cooking in oil used where possible? Yes/No
> Where fat is used in cooking, is it kept to a minimum? Yes/No
> Are unsaturated types of fat/oil used for   Yes/No
> cooking wherever possible?
> Are a variety of breads available?   Yes/No
> Are you encouraging healthier choices where   Yes/No
> there is more than a set meal available?
> Are children eating all the food they have?   Yes/No
> Which foods result in the highest waste?

From DfES Nutritional Guidelines at http://www.dfes.gov.uk/schoollunches/

A fistful of nuggets

Researchers in a study for Ofsted and the Food Standards Agency (FSA) have discovered that caterers in England supply 11 chicken nugget meals for every jacket potato.

Four times more biscuits than green vegetables (by weight) are eaten by the average boy in the UK.

Portly figures

Cost of a typical school dinner	40p
Cost of a typical can of dog food	47p
Percentage of packed lunchboxes containing crisps	71
Percentage of fat in a Big Mac	43.2
Percentage of fat in fried potato chips	36.5
Kcals in 100g of chips	253
Kcals in 100g of Big Mac	229
Kcals in one Big Mac	492

It was reported that some mass-produced bread loaves had so much added fat that three slices of bread contained more fat than a Mars Bar.

Where school lunch is the main reason to come to school

Boiled maize and beans is a life-saving daily school lunch for millions of children in western Kenya.

Children have to walk long distances to school, surviving at home on wild fruit, boiled for up to 12 hours to make it edible and clear it of poison. By the time they reach the school their energy levels are so low they can hardly read.

Food is the only motivation for walking long distances to school. It is such a strong incentive that many children start school before the required enrolment age, to benefit from the feeding programme.

From http://allafrica.com

Childhood obesity

Childhood obesity is a problem that has been around for 20 years but which has only been widely recognized in the last few years, says Dr John Reilly from the University of Glasgow:

> The epidemic started in the mid-1980s. We have seen very dramatic increases right through the 1990s, and all the signs suggest it is going to get worse before it gets better. . . The environment now promotes obesity in a way that it did not do before.

Obesity among the young is increasing as a result of children leading less active lifestyles. Children:

- watch more television
- play video games rather than playground games
- are taken to school by car rather than walking.

Also, more food has more calories and more fats: a McDonald's cheeseburger with fries and a shake require a nine-mile walk to burn off the calories.

European child obesity

A November 2003 Scottish report revealed:

One in five 12-year-olds is now classed as clinically obese.
One in ten Scots children aged 12 is classed as severely obese.
One in three Scots children aged 12 is overweight.
In England and in the US one in seven 15-year-olds is obese.

Overweight 12-year-olds in Europe:
France and Sweden 18 per cent
Germany 15 per cent
The Netherlands 13 per cent
Slovakia 10 per cent.

The Guardian, *September 2002, November 2003; Scientific Advisory Committee on Nutrition, 22 October 2003*

Bullying

Being fat is the most common cause of bullying.

The Times Educational Supplement, *28 May 2003*

Days of sickness

Canadian researchers have found that children with body fat higher than 25 per cent had significantly more days off school.

The illiterate of the year 2000 will not be those who cannot read and write, but those who cannot learn, unlearn and relearn. Our students need to be information literate, lifelong learners.

Toffler (1998)

A three-point analysis plan

P – Point (make your point succinctly).
E – Example (support your point with relevant examples).
E – Effect (describe the effect this point has on the reader).

Another three-point research plan

Preview
Do
Review.

The five-point study plan – SQ3R

Survey   (preview to get the general drift)
Question   (ask yourself questions about the content)
Read   (read it carefully)
Recall   (when you have read it, try to remember the main points)
Review   (go over the text again to check your understanding).

Big six

The Eisenberg/Berkowitz big six model of information problem-solving

1. *Task definition*
    1.1 Define the task (the information problem)
    1.2 Identify information needed in order to complete the task (to solve the information problem).
2. *Information seeking strategies*
    2.1 Brainstorm all possible sources
    2.2 Select the best sources.

3. *Location and access*
    3.1 Locate sources
    3.2 Find information within the source.
4. *Use of information*
    4.1 Engage in the source (read, hear, view, touch)
    4.2 Extract relevant information.
5. *Synthesis*
    5.1 Organize information from multiple sources
    5.2 Present the information.
6. *Evaluation*
    6.1 Judge the process (efficiency)
    6.2 Judge the product (effectiveness).

Eisenberg and Berkowitz (1990)

The nine-step plan

1. What do I need to do? (Formulate and analyse need.)
2. Where could I go? (Identify and appraise likely sources.)
3. How do I get to the information? (Trace and locate individual resources.)
4. Which resources shall I use? (Examine, select and reject individual resources.)
5. How shall I use the resources? (Interrogate resources.)
6. What should I make a record of? (Recording and sorting information.)
7. Have I got the information I need? (Interpreting, analysing, synthesizing, evaluating.)
8. How should I present it? (Presenting, communicating.)
9. What have I achieved? (Evaluation.)

From School Libraries: The Foundations of the Curriculum *(Office of Arts and Libraries/Working Party on School Library Services 1984)*

Surveying a book

Look at:

The cover What is the topic? The marketing angle? What does the graphic tell us? Can we estimate the likely audience using the colours, graphic, font style?

Title page What does the title suggest? Is the topic relevant to us? Do the author's name, experience and qualifications make it an informed book? Is it up to date?

Contents Focus on individual topics – is it what we are looking for? Ask simple questions – are the answers likely to be in here?

Introduction Is it relevant? Is the coverage and attitude what we are looking for?

Conclusion Does this summarize the topic adequately? Can we use the summary and then 'cherry pick' the rest of the book?

Index Focus on individual topics – is it what we are looking for? Ask simple questions – are the answers likely to be in here?

References and Bibliography Can this be used to follow up other sources of information?

Then start reading the main text.

How to spot a plagiarist

- Unusual fluency in a hitherto average pupil.
- Type five or six words from the essay into an Internet search engine and see if it matches an existing piece of work.
- Check for US spelling and vocabulary by an English pupil.
- Look out for unusual changes in font style, size or format.
- Look out for number references to texts which are not in a bibliography.
- Look out for references to unusual overseas publications.

Ways of discouraging plagiarism

At an early stage in the course:
- Set some work in examination conditions and retain it for purposes of comparison.
- Let it be widely known that you are doing the above.
- Teach a lesson on plagiarism and demonstrate how intelligent textual analysis can reveal inconsistencies.
- Openly discuss the merits of the grammar checkers and how a readability statistics feature can reveal individual written style.
- Make it a requirement that a pupil who word processes their work must show on demand: (a) preliminary drafts and notes,

(b) a digital copy of the work so it can be checked by a search engine and for readability statistics.
- Set work that is specific and relevant rather than conventional and copied from elsewhere. Copied questions generate copied responses!
- Require reference to specific topics, items, texts, etc.

Information statistics

(Relative rather than absolute)

Storage		
3000 BC	Clay tablets	1 character/1 cubic inch
AD 1450	Printed page	500 characters/cubic inch
1990s	Optical disk	125,000,000,000 cci
Computation		
5000 BC	Abacus	2–4 instructions per second
AD 1945	Computer	100 ips
1960s	Computer	100,000 ips
1970s	Computer	1,000,000 ips
1980s	Computer	10,000,000 ips
1990s	Computer	1,000,000,000 ips
Transmission of information		
4000 BC	Messenger	.01 words per minute
1844	Telegraph	50–60 words per minute
1980s	Cable/fibre	1,000,000,000 wpm
1990s	Fibre	100,000,000,000 wpm
Human information processing		
4000 BC	Written language	300 words per minute
1990s	Written language	300 words per minute
4000 BC	Visual images	100,000,000 bits per glance
1990s	Visual images	100,000,000 bits per glance
4000 BC	Spoken language	120 words per minute
1990s	Spoken language	120 words per minute

How can you remember?

According to the British Audio Visual Society, we remember about:
- 10 per cent of what we read
- 20 per cent of what we hear
- 30 per cent of what we see
- 50 per cent of what we see and hear
- 80 per cent of what we say
- 90 per cent of what we say and do at the same time.

School library/resources centres

	Mean	Median
Stock per pupil		
Fiction	4.7	3.5
Non-fiction	8.2	6.1
Additions		
Books per pupil	1.0	0.7
Other per 100 pupils	12.4	< 4
Issues per pupil		
Books	6.7	4.8
Other	0.27	0.02
Study places per 100 pupils	5.9	4.7
Expenditure per pupil	£6.62	£4.06

CILIP (2003)

School library staff

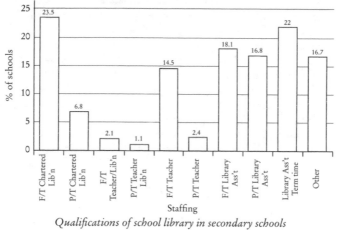

Qualifications of school library in secondary schools

CILIP (2003)

Whatever the costs of our libraries, the price is cheap compared to that of an ignorant nation.

Walter Cronkite

My two favourite things in life are libraries and bicycles. They both move people forward without wasting anything. The perfect day: riding a bike to the library.

Pete Golkin

Books can be dangerous. The best ones should be labeled 'This could change your life'.

Helen Exley

The greatest gift is the passion for reading. It is cheap, it consoles, it distracts, it excites, it gives you knowledge of the world and experience of a wide kind.

It is a moral illumination.

Elizabeth Hardwick

In the case of good books, the point is not to see how many of them you can get through, but rather how many can get through to you.

Mortimer J. Adler

David Milliband's five-point summary of personalized learning

1. *Assessment for learning* Using computer data to monitor individual progress, set targets and boost achievement.
2. Recognizing that pupils learn in different ways, at different speeds, and need to be taught how to learn. Individual and group learning can be helped by computer-mediated learning.
3. *Curriculum choice* Ability to choose individual pathways.
4. *The organization of learning in schools* The structure of the school day, timetables, buildings.
5. *Partnerships* With parents, business, the community, to support and encourage learning outside the classroom.

Milliband (2004)

Final products

Not every school task has to be an essay ...

art gallery, arts festival, autobiography, banner, book review, brochure, cartoon, collage, courtroom trial, debate, demonstration, diagram, diary, display case, exhibition, experiment, fact file, flag, flip chart, flow chart, game, heraldic shield, journal, letters, machine, magazine, model, mural, museum, musical instrument, picture book, puppet show, scrapbook, song, time capsule, time line, TV or radio commercial or advertisement, verdict, videotape.

Internet to blame?

Child pornography crimes rose by 1,500 per cent between 1988 and 2003.

Education epidemic

To transform schools we need networks and online communities of educators who are passionate about transferred innovation.

Government would not take control of it, administer it or even pay for it. Government would help it to flourish as a system that knows how to transfer innovation and best practice laterally and then simply gets on with the job.

In this way, education is like the Internet. It needs no central authority; nobody owns it, runs it, maintains it, or acts as a gatekeeper or regulator – and it works.

The Internet is both a vehicle for transformation and a model of how it might be done. We should be able to say the same of the innovation and best practice network in education.

Both systems could become 'peer-to-peer solutions to big problems'.

Hargreaves, (2003)

Technology as a bridge to learning

In his keynote speech at the 2001 BETT Conference Lord Puttnam of Queensgate said:

> I think it's become accepted that technology is, in itself, a bridge to learning rather than any kind of destination; and that a critical factor to the successful introduction of new learning tools is the intervention and involvement of a brilliant teacher.

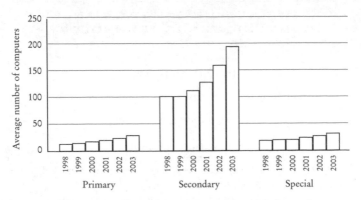

Average number of computers used mainly or solely for teaching and learning purposes per school: 1998–2003

The number of computers in schools increased each year from 1998 to 2003 for primary, secondary and special schools.

DfES (2003c)

How school websites have grown

Number of maintained primary schools with their own websites:	Number of maintained secondary schools with their own websites:
(1999): 3,800 (21 per cent)	(1999): 1,900 (54 per cent)
(2003): 10,200 (57 per cent)	(2003): 2,800 (82 per cent)

The first UK primary school website was published in 1994.

The first UK secondary school website was published on 1 February 1995 (Hinchingbrooke School, Huntingdon).

How much do you use ICT in your curriculum?

Percentage use of ICT in areas of the curriculum, 2003

Primary schools			
Subject	Substantial use	Some use	Little or no use
English	60	40	0
Maths	47	51	2
Science	24	71	5

Subject	Substantial use	Some use	Little or no use
English	19	69	12
Maths	31	57	11
Science	41	54	4

DfES (2003c)

How much do you spend on ICT?

Average expenditure per pupil on ICT in maintained schools, 2003

Primary schools	£56
Secondary schools	£69
Special schools	£259

All sectors showed expenditure that was up from 2001 but down from 2002.

DfES (2003c)

What effect does ICT have on learning?

The *ImpaCT2 report* by BECTA conclude that there is evidence that, taken as a whole, ICT can exert a positive influence on learning, though the amount may vary from subject to subject as well as between Key Stages, no doubt in part reflecting factors such as:

- the expertise of teaching staff;
- problems of accessing the best material for each subject at the required level; and
- the quality of ICT materials that are available.

How we can improve ICT effectiveness

A fundamental shift towards embedding ICT use across the curriculum:

- meaningful and authentic tasks
- developing skills within the curriculum rather than in discrete ICT lessons
- a greater emphasis on ICT use across all curriculum subjects
- centring upon the use of networked ICT in the classroom across the curriculum.

Higher levels and flexibility of:
- resourcing
- technical support
- staff development.

The following should also be considered:
- effective use of whiteboards
- uses and abuses of word processors
- ways of exploiting the potential of the Internet
- development of effective search and evaluation strategies
- ways to use resources to develop higher-order skills
- access to lightweight, portable ICT resources
- time to devote to ICT preparation and professional development
- funding for universal access
- auditing and increasing the levels of a school's use of ICT equipment
- hardware and software that are up to date, reliable and well maintained.

Schools should be aware of the increasing capabilities of many pupils, and allow for this in relation to the development of ICT skills.
Consider self-teaching packages for mixed ability pupils.
- Increase bandwidth.
- Use lightweight laptops and wireless networking.
- Encourage email and conferencing so pupils contact others for homework advice and support.
- Arrange electronic sharing of specialist teachers between schools.
- Match training to teachers' needs.
- Develop an evolving whole ICT school.
- Reappraise curriculum content and assessment practices to exploit the potential of ICT.

The role of ICT at home

Schools should:
Review the role of ICT-based homework for revision and self-directed projects.
Consider a more creative approach to homework.

Try to reduce the digital learning divide between home and school.

Carry out an audit of home computer ownership in order to target support.

Consider after-school and lunchtime access, and home loans of computers.

Aim for better communication about pupil computer use between home and school.

Play a significant role in disseminating models of good networked ICT practice.

Explain to parents the importance of home access of ICT and the potential learning that can occur.

Becta (2002)

ICT and managers

A hot air balloonist realizes he's lost, so reduces height to ask directions from a man on the ground.

'Excuse me, can you tell me where I am?'

'Yes,' says the man below. 'You're in a hot air balloon, hovering about 30 feet above this field.'

'You must work in Information Technology,' says the balloonist.

'I do,' replies the man. 'How did you know?'

'Well,' says the balloonist, 'everything you have told me is technically correct, but it's no use to anyone.'

The man below says, 'You must work in business as a manager.'

'I do,' replies the balloonist, 'but how did you know?'

'Well,' says the man, 'you don't know where you are, or where you're going, but you expect me to be able to help. You're in the same position you were before we met, but now it's my fault.'

Anon.

Digital Access Index 2002

The Digital Access Index (DAI) measures on a scale of 0 to 1 the overall ability of individuals in a country to access and use information and communications technology. It refers to five categories:

- Infrastructure (fixed and mobile phone subscribers)
- Affordability (Internet access price)
- Knowledge (adult literacy and school enrolment levels)

- Quality (bandwidth and subscribers)
- Users.

Results *(0 is minimum, 1 is maximum)*:

Sweden	0.85	UK	0.77
Denmark	0.83	Ireland	0.69
Iceland	0.82	South Africa	0.45
Canada, USA	0.78	Niger	0.04

Countries with 0.1 or less: Niger, Burundi, Guinea, Sierra Leone, Central African Republic, Ethiopia, Guinea-Bissau, Chad, Mali and Burkina Faso.

This reminds us that Internet *access* is not a global phenomenon, but yet another way of widening the divide between rich and poor nations.

International Telecommunication Union Report: http://www.itu.int

When Aids was audio-visual

Percentage of schools using audio-visual equipment (1974):

Record player	76.3 per cent
Mains tape recorder	79.8 per cent
Battery tape recorder	42.4 per cent
Filmstrip/slide/loop projector	57.3 per cent
Film projector	23.2 per cent
Television set	83.1 per cent
Radio	87.9 per cent.

DES (1975)

Checklist for creating distance learning resources

Is there appropriate motivation established to ensure student attention to the material and assignments?

Is the necessary content provided for all course components?

Is the presentation sequence of the content accurate and clearly indicated to guide students through the material?

Is all the required information available to the student in some format?

Do ample practice exercises exist for students to achieve appropriate rehearsal, processing, and knowledge acquisition of the content?

Are there adequate opportunities for instructor and classmate feedback included in the materials?

Are appropriate tests, activities and evaluation tools provided to assess student progress?

Are sufficient follow-through activities provided to maintain learning and motivation over time?

Is the student presented with clear paths, navigational guidance and transition information to direct them through the course material and components?

Are supplemental handouts, such as outlines or checklists, available to the student to facilitate transfer of learning provided?

Dick et al. *(2001)*

How to integrate multimedia resources into the classroom

Whole class
- Use a digital video projector onto a large screen.
- Use a large demonstration monitor placed high on a wall.
- Play a DVD on a DVD player instead of a computer.
- Use a networked computer room with enough terminals for at least two students per machine.

Small group
- Connect a TV screen to a computer.
- Use a desktop computer brought from elsewhere on a trolley.
- Use a laptop brought in for the purpose.

Other points
- Use curtains or blinds that 'dark out' rather than blackout or full light.
- Place monitors high and in a corner.
- If using laptops or trolleyed-in desktop computers check out: power sockets (how many, are they working, are they in the right place?)
  network sockets (one per computer, are they working, are they in the right place?)
  adequate broadband access (is it fast enough for your purpose, is it in the right place?).

- Avoid trailing leads; forbid movement between the machine and the wall.
- Arrange a rota of activities balanced between computer and non-computer, active and passive.
- Consider sending a small group outside the room if they can be overseen from the classroom.
- Explain clearly that everyone will have a chance to do this small group task.
- If using the Internet explain the rules concerning inappropriate access and concentrating on the task, not visiting irrelevant sites, etc.
- Make the task clear, relevant and with well-defined results.
- Networking CDs and DVDs can be a problem and may be expensive. The Internet is much easier for simultaneous access of a multimedia resource. However, Internet video quality is usually comparatively poor (speed of loading, size and quality of picture) even with Broadband.

Author

Interactive whiteboards 2002–3

92 per cent of secondary schools have at least one.
63 per cent of primary schools have at least one.
Average number per secondary school: 7.5.
Average number per primary school: 2.

The Times, *August 2004*

Great UK education websites

The DfES Standards site
http://www.standards.dfes.gov.uk/

Our goal is to improve the quality of teaching and learning throughout the system. We will do this by building capacity and providing flexibility at the front line, backed by an intelligent accountability framework and by targeted intervention to deal with underperformance.

The Research Informed Practice site
http://www.standards.dfes.gov.uk/research/

The aim of this site is to help teachers and parents make sure that practice and policy are informed by good and up-to-date evidence. It offers a searchable, electronic resource built principally from digests of recent papers from research journals.

Innovation Unit
http://www.standards.dfes.gov.uk/innovation-unit/

We want to be able to encourage and respond to innovative approaches to teaching and learning and school management from across the school system. Our goal is to ensure that schools are confident to innovate and change their practice to find solutions to learning challenges.

Numeracy Strategy
http://www.standards.dfes.gov.uk/numeracy/

The National Numeracy Strategy (NNS) supports teachers, trainee teachers and others working to improve numeracy in our primary schools.

Homework
http://www.standards.dfes.gov.uk/homework/

The examples of good practice on this site are intended to help schools develop, implement, and review their homework policies – as well as making available successful strategies for enlisting parental support.

Department for Education and Skills
http://www.dfes.gov.uk/index.htm

Main DfES site with information, resources and contacts for UK education.

Teachernet
http://www.teachernet.gov.uk/

Lesson plans, popular questions asked by teachers, links to expert help as well as pensions – this is the official teacher-oriented site.

National Grid for Learning (NGfL)
http://www.ngfl.gov.uk/

National Grid for Learning, the gateway to educational resources on the Internet. The NGfL provides a network of selected links to websites that offer high-quality content and information. Whether you are learning, supporting, teaching or managing, there are resources on the NGfL for you.

Qualifications and Curriculum Authority (QCA)
http://www.qca.org.uk/

QCA is a guardian of standards in education and training. We work with others to maintain and develop the school curriculum and associated assessments, and to accredit and monitor qualifications in schools, colleges and at work.

Office for Standards in Education
http://www.ofsted.gov.uk/

Our principal role is the management of the system of school inspection which provides for the regular inspection of all 24,000 state-funded schools in England. In addition to school inspections we undertake reviews of local education authorities, inspect initial teacher training courses, the nursery sector, independent schools and report on LEA-funded youth services.

National College for School Leadership
http://www.ncsl.org.uk/

Essential visiting for school leaders and others wanting up-to-the-minute background to education management issues, including candidates for the National Professional Qualification for Headship. Has links to relevant publications, essential leadership documents and discussion groups.

BBC Learning
http://www.bbc.co.uk/learning/

Learning for all, broadcast and online.

Becta

http://www.becta.org.uk/

Becta is the government's lead agency for ICT in education. Working to support the development of ICT in education throughout the UK, Becta's unique contribution is to combine knowledge of the needs of education with an understanding of the power of technology.

Teacher Training Agency

http://www.useyourheadteach.gov.uk/

Site encouraging people to become teachers. Essential site for recruitment and for providers of initial teacher training.

Governornet

http://www.governornet.co.uk/

Information for school governors.

Three cheers for the National Curriculum!

Physical training (1933)

Clothing

Where there is adequate changing accommodation the idea of the one layer garment and the right hygienic procedure can be carried out, but, as a rule, the poverty of the children and the lack of facilities at the school make a complete change of dress with a shower or a rub down after exercise impractical. Anyone who has critically watched a class attempting to perform exercises in coats, mufflers and perhaps even in hats, cannot fail to have realised the futility and absurdity of the proceeding.

The marking of playgrounds

Lump chalk rather than prepared chalk should be used, and in some districts pot or plate moulds thrown out from the factories can be obtained.

Games

In French Touch, if touched a player must hold the part of the body where he was touched and with this handicap chase the others.

When juggling with balls, children can amuse themselves by trying all kinds of tricks with balls.

Fundamental positions

The command 'attention' calls for a position of readiness and alertness from the class as a whole. It demands an attentive attitude of mind and a readiness to move in response to further directions. The constant practice of this position, rightly interpreted, cultivates in the children the ability to acquire and maintain good posture.

Board of Education (1933)

What very young children should experience

Looking after animals regularly
Taking part in nursery rhymes
Playing in groups at shops, fire stations, hospitals
Dressing up in groups
Caring for a younger child

Carrying out tasks that contribute to the life of the family on a
daily and weekly basis.

Brighouse (1999)

What's wrong with the National Curriculum?

Paul Francis suggested the following reasons in 1992. Are they still
true?

- It is politically, not educationally, motivated.
- It is imposed rather than agreed.
- It has not been openly discussed nor is it the product of
  consensus.
- It has too many aims and not enough vision.
- It is dominated by traditional subject headings.
- It is monolithic, rigid and poorly balanced in structure.
- It has no overall curriculum plan.
- It takes no account of school size, especially small schools.
- It has not been adequately resourced.
- It is overwhelmed by content and without overall coherence.
- It imposes impractical assessment.
- It leaves no room for development.

Adapted from Francis (1992)

Thomas Arnold's curriculum

At Rugby School, where he was appointed headmaster in 1827, the
forms were First, Second, Third, Lower Remove, Fourth, Upper
Remove, Lower Fifth, Fifth, Sixth.

First Form

Language	*Scripture*	*History*	*Maths*	*French*
Latin Grammar, Latin Delectus	Scriptural instruction, Church Catechism and Abridgement of New Testament, History.	Markham's *England* Vol. 1	Tables, Addition, Subtraction, Multiplication, Division (simple and compound), Reduction	Hamel's Exercises up to the Auxiliary verbs

Lower Remove

Scripture	History	Maths	French
Greek Grammar and Valpy's Exercises, Rule of the Greek Iambics, Easy parts of the Iambics of the Greek Tragedians, Virgil's *Eclogues,* Cicero de Senectute	St Matthew in Greek Testament, Acts in the English Bible	Parts of Justin, Parts of Xenophon's *Anabasis,* Markham's France to Philip of Valois	Hamel continued, Jussieu's *Jardin des Plantes*

Girls' education in Taleban Afghanistan

In 1998 the BBC announced that schools with girl pupils in Kabul, Afghanistan, had been closed down by the Taleban government.

The Taleban's Religious Affairs Minister, Haji Khulimuddin, said that the schools, believed to be teaching more than 3,000 girls, were closed because they 'were operating against the principles of Islamic law'.

The Taleban allow girls to receive an education only up to the age of eight, after which they have to leave school.

Training programmes which teach Afghan girls and women skills such as carpet weaving and other vocational skills have also been closed.

The Minister warned that anyone resisting this ruling would be punished.

We need boys ...

We need fine boys, boyish boys, who play the game gallantly and light-heartedly, who are never caddish or mean, who do their duty, stand for what is right and noble and good and true. We need boys who could not hit below the belt, however much they tried, who have an inborn sense of chivalry which prompts them naturally to be gentle towards women and girls, kindly to old folk, patient with the weak or handicapped, courteous in every deed and word.

Gee (1938)

Education isn't ...

An education isn't how much you have committed to memory, or even how much you know.

It's being able to differentiate between what you do know and what you don't. It's knowing where to go to find out what you need to know. And it's knowing how to use the information you get.

In times of change, learners shall inherit the earth while the learned, beautifully equipped for a world that no longer exists, perish.

Eric Hoffer

Know less. Understand more.

Anon.

Education is what remains, when what has been learned has been forgotten.

B.F. Skinner

Educating the mind without educating the heart is no education at all.

Aristotle

A good education should leave much to be desired.

Alan Gregg

I hear I forget
I see I remember
I do I learn
I reflect I improve

Kanwal I.S. Neel

How to transform education

Transformation requires everyone to learn: constantly, openly and quickly.

We must become adept at learning. We must become able not only to transform our institutions, in response to changing

Gone were the days when school assembly had been a hymn, a reading and a prayer!

situations and requirement; we must invent and develop institutions which are 'learning systems', that is to say, systems capable of bringing about their own continuing transformation.

Schön (1973)

Learning beyond the classroom

Alternatives to learning in the four walls of a classroom:
    community links
    community service
    partnership with industry
    partnership with other schools
    Internet-mediated collaboration and communication
    field trips and visits
    exchanges
    work experience
    video-conferencing
    extra-curricular sport and activities (Duke of Edinburgh Award
      Scheme, Change Makers)
    collaborative learning
    independent learning
    supported self-study
    cross-curricular 'collapsed timetable' activities.

Bentley (1998)

Practical maths problems

If the circumference of the driving wheel of a locomotive be $16\frac{1}{2}$ feet, how many revolutions will it make between Bristol and Exeter, the distance being $75\frac{1}{2}$ miles?

How many furlongs, rods, yards, feet and inches and Barley-corns will reach round the Earth, supposing it according to the best calculation to be 25,020 miles?

A rich nobleman has 5 villages, and in every village 3 streets, in every street 12 houses, in every house 5 rooms, in every room 2 Bureaus, in every Bureau 12 drawers, in every drawer 4 bags; every bag is valued at 150 guineas which he is going to exchange for £3.12s pieces. How many must he receive?

From a Suffolk school book c.1850, quoted in Evans (1956)

National Curriculum assessments of 7-,
11- and 14-year-olds in England, 2003

7-year-olds – Key Stage 1

Children reaching Level 2 or above:
- Reading task/test   84 per cent
- Writing   81 per cent (5 per cent less than 2002)
- Mathematics   90 per cent.

Children reaching Level 2B or above:
- Reading task/test   69 per cent
- Writing   62 per cent (2 per cent more than 2002)
- Mathematics   74 per cent (2 per cent less than 2002).

Girls outperform boys in all subjects at both levels.

At 16 percentage points, the gap is widest in writing at Level 2B or above.

Boys outperform girls by five points at Level 3 in maths.

11-year-olds – Key Stage 2

Children reaching Level 4 or above:
- English   75 per cent
- Reading   81 per cent
- Writing   60 per cent
- Mathematics   73 per cent
- Science   87 per cent.

Girls outperform boys in all aspects of English at Level 4 or above.

Boys outperform girls in maths at both Level 4 or above and at Level 5.

14-year-olds – Key Stage 3

Children reaching Level 5 or above:
- English   68 per cent
- Reading   68 per cent
- Writing   65 per cent

- Mathematics   70 per cent (a rise of 3 points on 2002)
- Science   68 per cent
- ICT teacher assessment 67 per cent.

How do we compare with Europe?

Mean scores of 15-year-olds, by EU country, 2000

	Reading	Mathematics	Science
Austria	507	515	519
Belgium	507	520	496
Denmark	497	514	481
Finland	546	536	538
France	505	517	500
Germany	484	490	487
Greece	474	447	461
Irish Republic	527	503	513
Italy	487	457	478
Luxembourg	441	446	443
Portugal	470	454	459
Spain	493	476	491
Sweden	516	510	512
United Kingdom	523	529	532

GCSE/GNVQ results

For pupils aged 15 in schools, 2002:

Percentage achieving 5 or more grades A*–C at GCSE/GNVQ: 52.6.

Percentage achieving 5 or more grades A*–G at GCSE/GNVQ: 88.6.

Percentage achieving 5 or more grades A*–G, including English and mathematics at GCSE/GNVQ: 86.3.

Percentage failing to achieve a pass at GCSE or the GNVQ equivalent: 5.4.

Percentage of girls failing to achieve 5 or more grades A*–C: 57.8.

Percentage of boys failing to achieve 5 or more grades A*–C: 47.5.

Girls continue to outperform boys, particularly at the higher grades.

In comprehensive schools

Percentage of pupils entered for 5+ GCSEs/GNVQs: 93.3.

Percentage achieving 5 or more grades A*–G at GCSE/GNVQ: 90.4.

Percentage achieving 5 or more grades A*–C: 50.1.

Percentage achieving 5 or more grades A*–G, including English and mathematics: 87.9.

Percentage achieving no passes: 3.8.

Government targets

Percentage of 16-year-old pupils to achieve 5 or more grades A*–G at GCSE/GNVQ, including English and mathematics by 2004: 92.

In 2001/2, 87.1 per cent achieved the target.

In 2002/3, 86.3 per cent achieved this target (a decrease of 0.8 per cent).

GCSE subject	% of 15-year-old pupils in all schools achieving A*–C in this subject	% of 15-year-old candidates attempting this subject achieving A*–C
English, Mathematics, Science and a Modern Foreign Language	28	40
English	56	60
Mathematics	48	51
Science	48	52
Design Technology	36	54
Modern Foreign Language	36	49
Classical Studies	2	86
Geography	20	61
History	20	63

GCSE/GNVQ results for young people in England,
DfES 2002/3 provisional figures

GCSE

The only comprehensive school with 100 per cent of pupils gaining five or more Grade C or above GCSEs in 2003 was a City Technology College – Thomas Telford School, Telford.

Over-examined

In June 2002 it was reported that some pupils had taken as many as 49 examinations in two years, including 10 GCSEs and 5 AS levels.

There were cases where pupils faced an exam timetable from 8am to 7pm – with some candidates taking up to four papers in a single day.

The exam overload can include . . .

Year 9 – English, maths, science standard assessment tests (typically two written exams each).

Year 11 – GCSEs (typically ten subjects with two written exams each).

Year 12 – AS levels (typically four to five subjects, three written examinations each).

Year 13 – A2s (typically three subjects, three written examinations each).

The cost of exams

Secondary schools are spending an average of £50,000 on entering students for A level, GCSE and vocational assessments. This is a 31 per cent increase in two years.

Additional costs are expected from September 2004 to pay for invigilators to administer exams.

It is estimated that the total cost to UK schools is more than £250 million.

The Times Educational Supplement, *25 June 2004*

Ten fallacies associated with testing

1 Tests measure ability.
2 Tests are predictive of future educational performance.
3 Tests are neutral in terms of gender and ethnicity.

4 Tests give parents accurate information about their children's progress.
5 Tests can be genuinely criteria based.
6 Tests allow the monitoring of standards over time.
7 Tests allow us to judge how good a school is.
8 Tests allow us to judge the national level of achievement against other countries.
9 Tests can be easily applied across the full range of educational experience.
10 Tests are essential to underpin a modern education system.

Moon (1999)

Examinations

In examinations the foolish ask questions that the wise cannot answer.

Oscar Wilde

Traditional knowledge

1. *To find the cost of a dozen articles*
   Reckon the cost of one article in pence, and then call the pence shillings.
   A farthing counts as 3d, and halfpenny as 6d.
   Thus 1 doz. articles at 1s 5¾d (17¾d) = 17¾s, i.e. 17s 9d.
   Reverse the process to find the cost of one article when given the cost of a dozen.
   Thus 13s 6d per dozen = 13½d each = 1s 1½d.
2. *To find the cost of a score of articles*
   Reckon every shilling as £1, and every penny as 1s 8d.
   Thus 1 score at 3s 4d each = £3 + (4 x 1s 8d), i.e. £3 6s 8d.

How many candidates take Classics?

O level Latin in 1960:   65,000
GCSE Latin in 2003:   10,000
GCSE Greek in 2003:   1,029
A level Greek in 2003:   263
AS level Greek in 2003:   246

Results in a sealed envelope are more humane than a public list

Town mouse, country mouse

Pupils who live in the country do better than pupils who come from the town:

Rural pupils with at least 5 GCSEs above grade C: 58.5 per cent.
Town pupils with at least 5 GCSEs above grade C: 46.7 per cent.

Rural pupils scoring above Level 4 in English at KS2: 79.4 per cent.
Town pupils scoring above Level 4 in English at KS2: 71.8 per cent.

Rural pupils scoring above Level 4 in Maths at KS2: 76.8 per cent.
Town pupils scoring above Level 4 in Maths at KS2: 70.9 per cent.

Rural pupils scoring above Level 4 in Science at KS2: 89.1 per cent.
Town pupils scoring above Level 4 in Science at KS2: 84.4 per cent.

The Times, *22 June 04*

AS levels

Teachers who said they were confident that they know the standard required for GCE AS: 81 per cent.
Teachers who said they were confident at A2: 76 per cent.
Teachers who said they were confident about VCE standards: 47 per cent.
Teachers who said they were confident that they had the skills to deliver key skills: 17 per cent.

'Considerable concerns' remain among schools and colleges about the overall assessment load for students between the ages of 14 and 19.

Teachers are committed to greater breadth at Level 3 – 36 per cent agreed.
Teachers are committed to the principle of greater flexibility at Level 3 – 40 per cent agreed.
Year 1 students are not coping well with their workload – 51 per cent; Year 2 students are coping – 73 per cent.
The amount of external assessment for GCE is about right – 27 per cent agreed, 42 per cent disagreed.
The amount of coursework in the GCE was about right: 45 per cent agreed, 25 per cent disagreed.

QCA (2003)

Are GCSE and A level standards being maintained?

QCA admits (April 2004):

- The change from a three- to a two-tier exam in science made it 'less effective'.
- There was an 'overall reduction in the knowledge and understanding content of syllabuses from all awarding bodies' by 2000.
- 'Revisions to the National Curriculum had deliberately lowered demand for exceptional performance'.
- By 2000, the lower-tier paper was 'significantly more demanding' for the less able.
- 'Extending the range of grades available on the higher-tier papers from B to A-star in 1995 to D to A-star in 2000 resulted in fewer questions requiring higher order skills'.
- 'Reviewers considered that these changes had resulted in a less effective assessment regime for both the least able and the most able candidates'.

Facts about A levels

1951: A levels were introduced – 37,000 candidates.

1963: Grades were introduced – top 10 per cent = A, bottom 30 per cent failed. This is called 'norm referencing', in which percentage passes are fixed.

At this time 15 per cent of 18-year-olds took A level.

Therefore an A at A level was limited to the top 1.5 per cent of a year group.

From 1982: pass numbers were increased.

1984: A grades are 9.3 per cent of passes.

1987: marking was changed to 'criteria referencing', in which any candidate reaching a given standard is awarded a grade.

Late 1990s: Curriculum 2000 reforms bring in AS levels, modular courses and coursework up to 25 per cent.

1993: A grades are 14.5 per cent of passes.

1998: A grades are 17.5 per cent of passes.

2001: A grades are 18.6 per cent of passes.

2002: A grades are 20.7 per cent of passes.

2003: A grades are 21.6 per cent of passes.

2004: A grades are 22.4 per cent of passes – 275,000 candidates.
Percentage of candidates achieving three or more A grades at
A level, 2003: 7.9.

The Sunday Times, *22 August 2004*

From A level to university

Number of applicants, 'nearly all' of whom were predicted straight
A grades at A level, turned down by Oxford and Cambridge:
2001–2: 8,000 approximately.
2003–4: more than 10,000.

Rise in number of first class degrees awarded by all UK universities:
1997–8: 19,472; 2002–3: 28,637 – a rise of 47.1 per cent.

Rise in total number of degrees in the same period: 9.1 per cent.
The Sunday Times, *18 April and 22 August 2004*

Examination answers (allegedly)

'The alimentary canal is located in the northern part of Indiana.'

'To keep milk from turning sour: keep it in the cow.'

'For drowning: climb on top of the person and move up and
down to make Artificial Perspiration.'

'The body consists of three parts – the brainium, the borax and
the abominable cavity. The brainium contains the brain, the borax
contains the heart and lungs, and the abominable cavity contains
the bowels, of which there are five – a, e, i, o and u.'

'The process of flirtation makes water safe to drink because it
removes large pollutants like grit, sand, dead sheep and canoeists.'

'A major disease associated with smoking is premature death.'

'I always know when it's time to get up when I hear my mother
sharpening the toast.'

What are steroids?
Things for keeping the carpet on the stairs.

Name the four seasons.
Salt, mustard, pepper, vinegar.

What is Britain's highest award for valour in war?
Nelson's Column.

'Sir Francis Drake circumcised the world with a 100 foot clipper.'

'The nineteenth century was a time of a great many thoughts and inventions. People stopped reproducing by hand and started reproducing by machine.'

'A rabbi is some body from a different village how has caught a diesese and would go to a oner place and give it to them.'

'A deluge is when you see something and it is not there.'

'A spinney is a woman who binds and makes things.'

'Two Communist countries are Ireland and Wales.'

Is this the worst exam question ever set about Shakespeare?

In *Macbeth*, Banquo warns Macbeth about the witches' influence. You give advice in a magazine for young people. You receive this request: 'Please advise me. I have recently moved school and made some new friends. I like spending time with them, but my form tutor thinks my work is suffering. What should I do?' Sam
Write your advice to be published in the magazine.

KS3 Shakespeare SAT question

Misbehaviour in examinations

More than 2,000 students had marks cancelled for breaking exam rules in 2002–3.

Disruptive exam behaviour:	464
Bringing mobile phones into exam room:	515
Other offences:	800.

The OCR Board reported an increase in misbehaviour of 400 per cent, and an increase in general exam rule breaking of 57 per cent.

Number of pupils the Boards took action against for colluding with others: 533 of 751 suspected.

Incidents included:
- making offensive comments on scripts (Edexcel, 67 cases)
- repeated disturbance (talking, tapping, throwing objects)
- confrontation with invigilators
- assaulting an invigilator
- appearing drunk and vomiting on the paper
- impersonation.

Six teachers were investigated by Edexcel for malpractice.

Two members of staff were banned from examining by OCR for tampering with students' coursework folders.

The Times Educational Supplement, *21 May 2004*

Victoria Crosses

Number awarded to Old Boys:

Eton	33
Harrow	20
Wellington	15
Cheltenham	14
Marlborough	12
Dulwich, Haileybury, Westminster, Stonyhurst	7 each

How many continue in education?

Total number of students in higher education:
    1965: 400,000
    2004: 2,000,000.

England

Young people going to university in England 2002–3: 44 per cent.
Young people going to university in England 1999–2000: 41 per cent.
Government target: 50 per cent of all under-30s into higher
    education by 2010.

Females at university: 47 per cent.
Males at university: 40 per cent.

Office for National Statistics (2002)

UK student numbers

In the 1950s only 50,000 students per year went to university.
    Between 1979 and 1997 …
    the number of full-time university students doubled.
    the amount the government paid the universities per student was
        cut in half.
    staff–student ratios fell from 1:9 to 1:17.

    Higher Education (HE) refers to an academic level above GCE
        A level.
    Further Education (FE) refers to an academic level below GCE
        A level.

Total in higher education (1965 – 2001)

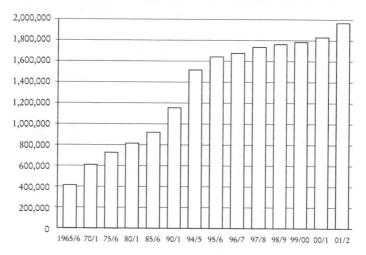

Higher education trends, 2003: number of students in the UK

Published in The Times Higher Education Supplement, *19 September 2003*

25.2 per cent of all postgraduate students were from overseas.
52.9 per cent of first-year undergraduates of known age were 21 or over.
Total income of all UK higher education institutions in 2001–2 was £14.5 billion.
Women overtook men as a proportion of the undergraduate population in 1996–7.

The Times Higher Education Supplement,
19 September 2003

First class degrees awarded

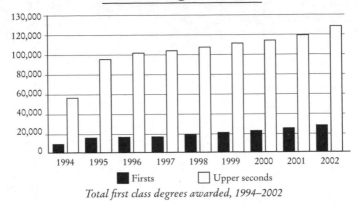

Total first class degrees awarded, 1994–2002

HESA, published in The Times Higher Education Supplement,
19 September 2003

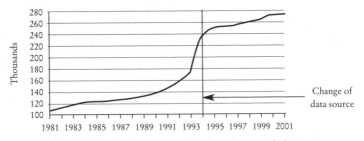

The number of first degrees awarded has almost tripled in 20 years

Source: DfEE (1981–93), HESA (1994 onwards), published in The Times
Higher Education Supplement, *19 September 2003*

Universities in the olden days ...

Number of universities in 1963:   31.
Number of universities in 2004:   100.

Universities	Full-time undergraduates 1900	Full-time undergraduates 2000
Aberystwyth	474	5,500
Bangor	279	5,408
Birmingham	331	13,905
Bristol	336	9,989
Cambridge	3,126	11,627
Cardiff	500	3,329
Durham	182	9,167
Edinburgh	2,354	15,604
Glasgow	1,921	14,820
King's College London	274	12,228
Leeds	580	17,904
Liverpool	481	10,946
London School of Economics	48	3,384
Manchester	861	16,836
Nottingham	227	13,349
Oxford	2,776	10,993
Reading	106	7,615
Sheffield	96	13,242
Southampton	195	12,803
St Andrews	351	4,965
University College London	462	10,694

Hall and Haywood (2001); Hindmarsh et al. *(2004)*

Vice-chancellors' pay

The highest paid vice-chancellor was L. Tyson of the London Business School, who earned £315,000 in 2002/3.

The norm was around £130,000.

The Times Higher Education Supplement, *20 February 2004*

Degrees for women

Oxford University allowed women to be members of the university, and therefore to receive degrees, in 1920.

Cambridge University finally offered full degrees to women in 1948.

Most applications

These universities are the most popular with potential students:

1.	Leeds	50,266
2.	Nottingham	50,148
3.	Manchester	47,725
4.	Bristol	37,609
5.	Manchester Metropolitan	37,442
6.	Birmingham	36,794
7.	Ulster	31,686
8.	Edinburgh	31,466
9.	Warwick	31,117
10.	Sheffield	30,969

Hindmarsh et al. *(2004)*

Universities abroad

International university participation rates:
New Zealand: 76 per cent
Australia: 65 per cent
Finland: 72 per cent
Hungary: 56 per cent
Netherlands: 54 per cent.
Argentina: 59 per cent
Philippines: 52 per cent.

BBC: www.bbc.co.uk

An unqualified success

Proof you can be successful without university qualifications:
John Caudwell (engineering, £1,280 million)
Trevor Hemmings (bricklaying, £700 million)
Laurence Graff (jewellery, £450 million)
Jim McColl (engineering, £330 million)

John Frieda (hair care, £170 million)
Sir Stan Clarke (plumbing, £148 million)
Sir David McMurty (Rolls-Royce, engineering, £148 million)
Alexander McQueen (tailoring, £20 million)
Karen Millen (fashion, £20 million)
Jamie Oliver (cookery, £20 million)
Gordon Ramsey (football, catering, £20 million)

The Times, *19 June 2004*

Largest university building

MV Lomonosov Moscow State University: 32 storeys and 40,000 rooms.

Cambridge Colleges and date of foundation

Cambridge University was founded by scholars from Oxford. The first record is in 1209.

Peterhouse	1284	Homerton	1768
Clare	1326	Downing	1800
Pembroke	1347	Girton	1869
Gonville & Caius	1348	Newnham	1871
Trinity Hall	1350	Selwyn	1882
Corpus Christi	1352	Hughes Hall	1885
King's	1441	St Edmund's	1896
Queens'	1448	New Hall	1954
St Catharine's	1473	Churchill	1960
Jesus	1496	Darwin	1964
Christ's	1505	Lucy Cavendish	1965
St John's	1511	Wolfson	1965
Magdalene	1542	Clare Hall	1966
Trinity	1546	Fitzwilliam	1966
Emmanuel	1584	Robinson	1977
Sidney Sussex	1596		

Taylor (1994)

Oxford Colleges, date of foundation, alumni

All Souls	1438	Sir Christopher Wren, T.E. Lawrence
Balliol	1263	John Wyclif, Gerard Manley Hopkins, Robert Southey, Matthew Arnold, H.H. Asquith, Harold MacMillan, Edward Heath, Roy Jenkins, Denis Healey, Aldous Huxley, Graham Greene
Brasenose	1509	Field Marshal Earl Haig, Jeffrey Archer, John Buchan, William Golding, Michael Palin, Robert Runcie
Christ Church	1526	Sir Philip Sidney, Robert Hooke, William Penn, John Wesley, C.L. Dodgson (alias Lewis Carroll), William Walton, W.H. Auden, Auberon Waugh, David Dimbleby, and 14 British prime ministers including Robert Peel, William Gladstone and Anthony Eden
Corpus Christi	1517	Thomas Arnold, John Keble, John Ruskin
Exeter	1314	Hubert Parry, William Morris, J.R.R. Tolkein, Richard Burton, Roger Bannister, Alan Bennett
Hertford	1282	William Tyndale, John Donne, Jonathan Swift, Evelyn Waugh, Henry Pelham
Jesus	1571	T.E. Lawrence, Harold Wilson, Magnus Magnussen
Keble	1870	Peter Pears, Imran Khan
Lady Margaret Hall	1878	Baroness Warnock, Lady Antonia Fraser, Benazir Bhutto
Lincoln	1427	Howard Florey, Edward Thomas, John Le Carré, Dr Seuss

Magdalen	1458	Cardinal Wolsey, C.S. Lewis, John Betjeman, Oscar Wilde, Dudley Moore
Merton	1264	John Wyclif, Thomas Bodley, Lord Randolph Churchill, Max Beerbohm, T.S. Eliot, Kris Kristopherson
New	1379	Rev. William Spooner, John Galsworthy, Hugh Gaitskell, Tony Benn
Oriel	1326	Sir Walter Raleigh, Cecil Rhodes, Edward Pusey, Cardinal Newman, Beau Brummell, John Keble, A.J.P. Taylor
Pembroke	1624	Samuel Johnson, James Lewis Smithson, Michael Heseltine, William Fulbright
The Queen's	1341	King Henry V, Edmund Halley, Rowan Atkinson, Brian Walden
Somerville	1879	Indira Gandhi, Dorothy L. Sayers, Iris Murdoch, Margaret Thatcher
St Edmund Hall	1278	Terry Jones, Sir Robin Day
St John's	1555	Edmund Campion, William Laud, Robert Graves, A.E. Houseman, John Wain, Kingsley Amis, Philip Larkin, Tony Blair
Trinity	1555	William Pitt the Elder, George Calvert, Jeremy Thorpe, Terence Rattigan, Anthony Crossland, James Elroy Flecker, Laurence Binyon
University	1249	Robert Boyle, Percy Bysshe Shelley, C.S. Lewis, Dr John Radcliffe, Clement Attlee, Bill Clinton, Willie Rushton, Richard Ingrams, Bob Hawke, Stephen Hawking

Wadham	1610	Sir Christopher Wren, Sir Thomas Beecham, Cecil Day-Lewis, Michael Foot, Melvyn Bragg
Worcester	1714	Richard Adams, Rupert Murdoch, John Sainsbury
+ 21 other Halls and Colleges		

Challenging Oxbridge interview questions

What is the effect on the whole of society if someone crashes into a lamp-post? (Law)

Are people living on the streets mad if they can sing? (PPE)

Give an example of two statements that can't both be true but can both be false, and two statements that can't both be true and can't both be false (Philosophy)

Would a good liar make a good lawyer? (Law)

Why don't plants have brains? (Veterinary Science)

Is the Eurovision Song Contest an example of living nationalism? (History & Politics)

Could there still be a Second Coming if mankind had disappeared from the planet? (Theology)

How do you know if 2 + 2 = 4 in the past? (Philosophy)

What would you say if I told you that you have more than the average number of legs? (Mathematics)

The Oxford College with the longest name

Oriel College is officially known as 'The Provost and Scholars of the House of the Blessed Mary the Virgin in Oxford, commonly called Oriel College, the foundation of Edward the Second of famous memory, sometime King of England'.

Oxford information at http://www.oxford-info.com

Durham University Colleges

Collingwood	St John's
George Stephenson	St Mary's
Grey	Trevelyan
Hatfield	University College
John Snow	Ushaw
St Aidan's	Ustinov
St Chad's	Van Mildert
St Cuthbert's Society	Teikyo University in Durham
College of St Hild & St Bede	

Independent schools pre-1500 and foundation date

England

The King's School, Canterbury	597
(by St Augustin)	
St Peters School, York	627
(by Paulinus)	
Warwick School, Warwick	914
King's School, Ely	970
(Edward the Confessor was a pupil here;	
school reconstituted in 1541 by Henry VIII)	
St Albans School, Hertfordshire	1100
(monastic foundation 948)	
Wells Cathedral School, Somerset	1150
Abingdon School, Oxfordshire	1256
Royal Grammar School, Worcester	1291
Bablake School, Coventry	1344
Wisbech Grammar School	1379
Winchester College	1382
(by William of Wykeham)	
Hereford Cathedral School, Hereford	1384
Ipswich School, Suffolk	1390
Oswestry School, Shropshire	1407
Durham School, Durham	1414
Sevenoaks School, Kent	1432
Eton College, Berkshire	1440

King's College School, Cambridge (by Henry VI)	1441
City of London School, London	1442
St Dunstan's College, London	1446
Magdalen College School, Oxford	1480
Stockport Grammar School, Cheshire	1487
Loughborough Grammar School, Leicester	1495

Scotland

High School of Glasgow	1124
High School of Dundee	1239

University league tables – the main indicators

A-level points The average number of UCAS points held by first-year students

Applications vs. places The total number of applications to degree courses against the total number accepted. This indicates how competitive it is to get onto the course

Student:staff ratio On average, the number of staff in relation to the number of students

Teaching The marks received in teaching assessments by individual departments

Research The research rating received by each department

Degree classifications Firsts and upper Seconds as a percentage of all classified degrees

Employment The percentage of graduates entering full-time employment

Drop-out rate The percentage of students failing to complete courses

Library and computer spending

Undergradually

England

Proportion of under-30s entering higher education in 1988: 12 per cent.

Proportion of under-30s entering higher education in 2003: 43 per cent.

Proportion of under-30s entering higher education in 2004: 44 per cent.

Government target for under-30s into higher education by 2010: 50 per cent.

Proportion of undergraduates achieving a first or upper second in 1998: 49.5 per cent.

Proportion of undergraduates achieving a first or upper second in 2003: 58.2 per cent.

Scotland

Percentage of 17–21-year-olds in higher education in 2001–2: 51.9.

Northern Ireland

Percentage of 18–30-year-olds in higher education: 50.

Other countries

New Zealand: 76 per cent.
Finland: 72 per cent.
Australia: 65 per cent.
Argentina: 59 per cent.
Hungary: 56 per cent.
Netherlands: 54 per cent.
The Philippines: 52 per cent.

Higher education funding

- Funding per student fell 36 per cent between 1989 and 1997.
- 87 per cent of students agree that university is a good investment.
- Those with an HE qualification are likely to earn on average 50 per cent more than those without.

- By 2010 the number of jobs requiring the sorts of skills that can be acquired through HE will grow by 1.73 million – that's 80 per cent of new jobs created over the next decade.
- Graduates are 50 per cent less likely to be unemployed than non-graduates.
- Graduates earn, on average, significantly more than non-graduates. Young graduates aged 21–30 can expect to earn £6,500 more each year than non-graduates in the same age bracket.

Higher Education, DfES

How many graduate jobs?

Brown and Hesketh (2004):	*Government:*
Three years after graduating 40% of recent graduates are in jobs that do not require degree-level skills	80% of the 1.7 million jobs expected to be created by 2010 will require degree-level qualifications
Starting salaries for graduates are falling, with the average for 2003 of £12,659 substantially lower than the £13,422 in 2002	The average salary of those leaving university is expected to rise by 3.9% in 2004 to £21,000
20% of workers have a job that makes use of degree-level qualifications	40% of Britain's labour force will be in 'knowledge-based' employment by 2005
The number of 'blue chip' (defined as well-paid, esteemed and interesting) jobs has fallen from 25,000 in 1997 to 21,500 in 2003	
Only 5% of new graduates will be employed in blue chip jobs	

The Times, *29 March 2004*

Most higher education institutes

Mexico: 10,341.

Foreign students flood in

British Council figures show:

Non-EU international student numbers rose by 32,000 or 23 per cent in 2003.

The intake from China and India rose by 80 per cent.

174,575 overseas students studied in the UK in 2002–3.

A further 95,515 were from the EU.

Universities can make more than £5,000 profit for each foreign student.

Further education colleges

Number of further education colleges in the UK in 2001–2: 483
Number of full-time lecturers in FE institutions: 56,000

Sir Bulwer Lytton's advice to Glasgow University students

Learn to say 'no' with decision; 'yes' with caution.

'No' with decision whenever it meets a temptation.

'Yes' with caution whenever it implies a promise.

A promise given is a bond inviolable. A man is already of consequence in the world when we know we can implicitly rely on him. I have frequently seen such a man preferred to a long list of applicants for some important charge; he has been lifted at once into station and fortune merely because he has this reputation: that when he says he knows a thing he knows it; and when he says he will do a thing he will do it.

Names of Gormenghast teachers

Fluke	Shrivell
Spiregrain	Shimmer
Perch-Prism	Cutflower
Splint	Deadyawn
Throd	Bellgrove
Flannelcat	Mulefire
Shred	Crust

Peake (1970)

Names of Greyfriars teachers

Dr Locke (Headmaster)
Mr Prout (master of the Fifth)
Mr Hacker (master of the Shell)
Mr Quelch (master of the Remove)
Mr Lascelles (master of Mathematics and Games)
M. Charpentier (master of French)

The Greyfriars stories by Frank Richards

Names of Gormenghast pupils

Parsley	Dankle
Chives	Dogseye
Tinepott	Slypate
Quagfire	Smattering
Sparrowmarsh	Scarabee
Hagg	Mint

Peake (1970)

Names of Greyfriars students (The Remove)

Bolsover, Percy (Major)
Brown, Tom
Bull, John
Bulstrode, George
Bunter, William George (Major)
Cherry, Robert
Delarey, Piet
Desmond, Michael
Dupont, Napoleon
Dutton, Tom
Field, Sampson Quincy Iffley
Fish, Fisher Tarleton
Hazeldene, Peter
Hillary, Richard
Kipps, Oliver
Linley, Mark
Mauleverer, The Rt Hon. The Earl of
Morgan, David
Newland, Montague
Nugent, Frank (Major)
Ogilvy, Donald Robert
Penfold, Richard
Rake, Richard
Redwing, Tom
Russell, Richard
Singh, Hurree Jamset Ram (H.R.H. the Nabob of Bhanipur)
Skinner, Harold
Smith, Robert Fortescue (Minor)
Snoop, Sidney James
Stott, William
Todd, Peter Hastings
Treluce, Anthony
Trevor, Herbert Beauchamp
Vernon-Smith, Herbert Tudor
Vivian, Sir James (Bart)
Wibley, William Ernest
Wun Lung

The Greyfriars stories by Frank Richards

Members of Hogwarts

Professors

Binns	History of Magic
Albus Dumbledore	Headmaster
Flitwick	Charms
Rubeus Hagrid	Gamekeeper/Care of Magical Creatures
Minerva McGonagall	Transfiguration
Sinistra	Astronomy
Severus Snape	Potions
Sprout	Herbology
Sibyll Trelawney	Divination
Vector	Arithmancy

Teachers of Defence against the Dark Arts

Quirrel
Gilderoy Lockhart
Remus Lupin
Alastor 'Mad-eye' Moody
Dolores Umbridge

Other instructors

Madam Hooch	Quidditch Instructor
Madam 'Poppy' Pomfrey	Nurse
Madam Pince	Librarian
Firenze	Divination
Argus Filch	Caretaker

Harry Potter series by J.K. Rowling

Pupils by House (selective, excluding former pupils)

Gryffindors

Harry Potter, Hermione Granger, Ron Weasley, Katie Bell, Lavender Brown, Colin Creevey, Dennis Creevey, Seamus Finnigan, Angelina Johnson, Lee Jordan, Neville Longbottom, Natalie McDonald, Parvati Patil, Alicia Spinnet, Dean Thomas, Fred Weasley, George Weasley, Ginny Weasley.

Ravenclaws

Stewart Ackerly, Terry Boot, Mandy Brocklehurst, Cho Chang, Padma Patil, Orla Quirke, Lisa Turpin.

Hufflepuffs

Hannah Abbot, Susan Bones, Eleanor Branstone, Owen Cauldwell, Justin Flinch-Fletchley, Ernie MacMillan, Kevin Whitby.

Slytherins

Malcolm Baddock, Millicent Bulstrode, Vincent Crabbe, Gregory Goyle, Draco Malfoy, Pansy Parkinson, Graham Pritchard, Blaise Zabini.

Harry Potter series by J.K. Rowling

Characterful pupils in literature

Spadge Hopkins, *In Cider With Rosie* by Laurie Lee, who, too old for his country school – 'The sight of him squeezed into his tiny desk was worse than a bullock in ballet-shoes' – was goaded once too often by his teacher, 'Crabby B'. He lifted her to the top of a cupboard and left her there as he quit the school.

Who were the Famous Five?

Enid Blyton wrote 21 original stories featuring the Famous Five, who were:

Julian, Dick, Anne, George, Timmy/Timothy.
George's parents were Quentin and Frances.

Story titles	Dates published by Hodder & Stoughton
Five on a treasure island	Sept 1942
Five go adventuring again	July 1943
Five run away together	Oct 1944
Five go to Smuggler's Top	Oct 1945
Five go off in a caravan	Nov 1946
Five on Kirrin Island again	Aug 1947
Five go off to camp	Oct 1948
Five get into trouble	Oct 1949
Five fall into adventure	Sept 1950
Five on a hike together	Sept 1951
Five have a wonderful time	Sept 1952
Five go down to the sea	Sept 1953
Five go to mystery moor	July 1954
Five have plenty of fun	July 1955
Five on a secret trail	July 1956
Five go to Billycock Hill	July 1957
Five get into a fix	July 1958
Five on Finniston Farm	July 1960
Five go to Demon's Rocks	July 1961
Five have a mystery to solve	July 1962
Five are together again	July 1963

Some were originally serialized in *Princess* magazine.

http://www.btinternet.com/~ajarvis/blyton/five.htm

Who were the Secret Seven?

There were 15 books in Enid Blyton's Secret Seven series.

The Secret Seven were: Peter, Janet, Pam, Colin, George, Jack, Barbara and Scamper.

Enid Blyton

Enid Blyton, probably the most successful British children's writer of the twentieth century, was born in London on 11 August 1897 and died in 1968.

Who were William's Outlaws?

William Brown, Ginger, Douglas and Henry.
The bane of William's life is Violet Elizabeth Bott.
William's sister is Ethel, his older brother is Robert.

How William's life reflects changing times

The books were published over several decades, from the 1920s through the depression, the Second World War, and into the post-war era.

Late 1920s – William's house started as a mansion with stables and summer houses.

By the 1930s the Brown home had shrunk to a middle-class suburban semi-detached house. The large domestic staff of cook, housemaid and gardener during the 1920s were replaced by a daily.

Richmal Crompton

The real name of Richmal Crompton, author of the William stories, was Richmal Crompton Lamburn. (Born 1890 in Bury in Lancashire, died 1969.)

At the age of 27 she had become a senior Classics mistress at a girls' school in Bromley, south east London. She contracted poliomyelitis (polio) in 1923. She was left without the use of her right leg and was lame for the remainder of her life. William first appeared in a story called 'Rice Mould' in *The Ladies Home Magazine* in 1919 and was published eventually in 400 stories in 38 books. The first book was *Just William* (1922); the last was *William the Superman* (1968).

The William Stories by Richmal Crompton

Who wrote Jennings and Darbishire?

Anthony Buckeridge (1912–2004) had the first story serialized on radio in 1948 and *Jennings Goes to School*, the first of 22 books, came out two years later.

John Christopher Timothy Jennings and his friend Darbishire attend Linbury Court Boys' Preparatory School in Dunhambury, Sussex. The books also featured Venables, Bromwich, Atkinson and the master Mr Wilkins.

Buckeridge attended a Prep school as a boy and taught at St Laurence's, Ramsgate where he created stories for the boys.

The Jennings Stories by Anthony Buckeridge

Characters in *Stalky and Company* by Rudyard Kipling

Stalky, M'Turk, Beetle
Mr Prout, Foxy, Mr Hartopp.

Leanne by any other name ...

A behaviour support worker noted that her referral list has 'very few Elizabeths and Timothys, several Kyles, lots of Charlenes and Kylies, spelt in many ways'.

Other research shows that Victoria will nearly always gain higher marks than Leanna.

Top 20 names for children born in 2003

	Girls	*Boys*
1.	Emily	Jack
2.	Ellie	Joshua
3.	Chloe	Thomas
4.	Jessica	James
5.	Sophie	Daniel
6.	Megan	Oliver
7.	Lucy	Benjamin
8.	Olivia	Samuel
9.	Charlotte	William
10.	Hannah	Joseph
11.	Katie	Harry
12.	Ella	Matthew
13.	Grace	Lewis
14.	Mia	Luke
15.	Amy	Ethan
16.	Holly	George
17.	Lauren	Adam
18.	Emma	Alfie
19.	Molly	Callum
20.	Abigail	Alexander

Old Boys and Girls

Durham Choristers Prep School: Tony Blair, Rowan Atkinson

Godolphin & Latymer School: Nigella Lawson, Davina McCall

Wimbledon College: Paul Merton, John Patten

Westminster School: Peter Ustinov, Tony Benn, Imogen Stubbs, Andrew Lloyd Webber

Brentwood: Douglas Adams, Jack Straw, Noel Edmonds, Griff Rhys-Jones

Rugby: Salman Rushdie, Chris Brasher, Andrew Rawnsley, Robert Hardy

North London Collegiate: Esther Rantzen, Eleanor Bron

Leeds Grammar: Barry Cryer, Gerald Kaufman

Badminton: Iris Murdoch, Claire Bloom, Indira Gandhi

Birkdale: Michael Palin, Rex Harrison

Wellington: Keith Floyd, Jeffrey Archer

Radley: Peter Cook, Brough Scott, Ted Dexter

Clifton: John Cleese, John Inverdale, Chris Serle

The Leys: Alastair Burnett, Martin Bell

The Mount: Judi Dench, Margaret Drabble

Nottingham High: Kenneth Clarke, Lesley Crowther

Marlborough: Chris de Burgh, Mark Phillips

Haileybury: Stirling Moss, Alan Ayckbourn

Rutlish School: John Major, Raymond Briggs

Highgate: Geoffrey Palmer, Barry Norman, Phil Tufnell

The Perse: David Gilmour, Peter Hall

Dulwich College: P.G. Wodehouse, Raymond Chandler, Bob Monkhouse

Charterhouse: Jonathan King, David Dimbleby, Peter Gabriel

Bootham: A.J.P. Taylor, Brian Rix

Manchester Grammar: Ben Kingsley, Robert Powell, Mike Atherton

Eton: Sir Robert Walpole, Robert Hartley, William Pitt the Elder, Horace Walpole, the Duke of Wellington, Thomas Gray, Percy Bysshe Shelley, William Ewart Gladstone, William Webb-Ellis.

Educated at home

(At least part of the time)

Albert Einstein, Noel Coward, Irving Berlin, Felix Mendelssohn, Wolfgang Amadeus Mozart, Thomas Edison, Orville and Wilbur Wright, Agatha Christie, Yehudi Menuhin, C.S. Lewis, Alexander Graham Bell, Elizabeth II, G.B. Shaw, Claude Monet, Mark Twain, Hans Christian Andersen, Charlie Chaplin, Benjamin Franklin, John Stuart Mill, Albert Schweitzer, Leo Tolstoy, John Wesley.

US Presidents educated at home

George Washington (1st), Thomas Jefferson (3rd), Abraham Lincoln (16th), Woodrow Wilson (28th), Franklin D. Roosevelt (32nd).

Expelled from school

Martin Amis (bunking)
Roger Daltrey (smoking and refusing to wear uniform)
Boy George (bunking)
Jackie Collins (smoking)
Jade Jagger (bunking off to see a boyfriend)
Stephen Fry (theft)
Jeremy Clarkson (accumulated misdemeanours)
Benjamin Zephaniah (aged 13).

School choice

Number of appeals by parents unhappy with the choice of schools: 70,000, equivalent to 10 per cent of 11-year-olds.

Pupils wanting to attend Lauriston Primary in Hackney need to live within 150 yards of its door.

Pupils wanting to attend Fortismere Comprehensive in north London have to live within a mile of the school.

Number of parents claiming they would use dishonest methods to get their child into a school: 29 per cent.

The Sunday Times, *13 June 2004*

Ways to try to get your child into an oversubscribed school

Appeal to a tribunal (33 per cent success rate)

Move into catchment area

Buy a flat in the catchment area and claim that as your address

Send child to live with relative or friend living in catchment area

Falsify your address

Claim strong religious beliefs (for religious foundation schools)

Send another, cleverer, child to sit entrance exam in your child's name

Bribe head teacher (offer contributions to funds, free IT equipment, use of holiday home …)

Claim relationship with sibling already at the school

Apply for job as teacher of a shortage subject and insist your child is allowed to attend too.

Families

Children living in a family with two parents (UK, 1981): nine out of ten.

Children living in a family with two parents (UK, 2001): eight out of ten.

Children living in a lone parent family (UK, 1981): 12 per cent.

Children living in a lone parent family (UK, 2001): 20 per cent.

Proportion of lone parent families headed by a Black person, or someone of mixed origin: 40 per cent.

Proportion of lone parent families headed by an Asian person: 10 per cent.

Office for National Statistics (2002)

Bereavement

- Every 30 minutes, somewhere in Britain, a child under 18 is bereaved of a parent.
- 20,000 children are bereaved every year.

The Child Bereavement Trust

Sex

The percentage of 15-year-old girls who said they had had sexual intercourse:

Greece, Poland, Israel: 10 per cent.

Wales, England, Greenland: 40 per cent.

WHO (2004)

Age limits

At this age you can …

Age 12 Buy a pet

Age 13 Do a part-time job

Age 16 Hold a licence for a moped or motorbike under 50 cc

          Buy and smoke cigarettes

          Buy fireworks

          A girl can have sexual intercourse

          Change your name with parental consent

          Get married with parental consent

          Apply for a passport with parental consent

Age 17 Hold a licence for a car or motorbike

Age 18 Get married

          Open a bank account

          Apply for a passport

          Vote in an election

          Get a tattoo

          Buy and consume alcohol in public

Pre-school

The Pre-school Playgroups Association was set up to provide for under-fives in 1962.

Facts or discovery?

The teaching of English should not be about a 'voyage of self-discovery' for children. It is about the use of a tried and tested approach that involves the teaching of a set body of knowledge.

John Patten, Education Secretary 1992

Thomas Gradgrind, sir. A man of realities. A man of fact and calculations. A man who proceeds upon the principle that two and two are four, and nothing over, and who is not to be talked into allowing for anything over. Thomas Gradgrind, sir – peremptorily Thomas – Thomas Gradgrind. With a rule and a pair of scales, and the multiplication table always in his pocket, sir, ready to weigh and measure any parcel of human nature, and tell you exactly what it comes to. It is a mere question of figures, a case of simple arithmetic. You might hope to get some other nonsensical belief into the head of George Gradgrind, or Augustus Gradgrind or John Gradgrind, or Joseph Gradgrind (all suppositions, non-existent persons), but into the head of Thomas Gradgrind – no sir!

From Hard Times, *Charles Dickens (first published 1854)*

The important thing is not so much that every child should be taught as that every child should be given the wish to learn.

Sir John Lubbock, 1834–1913

Orwell's *1984* describes Newspeak, a language whose purpose is to reduce the vocabulary and range of language which in turn narrows down the range of thought. So 'thoughtcrime' becomes literally impossible.

The notion of something becoming unthinkable is the antithesis of creativity.

Author

The government's education reforms have constantly stressed the devolution of power while steadily increasing ministerial authority. The Education Reform Act for all its concerns with individual schools to run their own affairs, still gave the Secretary of State 464 extra powers. Its premise was that standards would be levered up if schools had to introduce reforms such as the National Curriculum and testing, but good schools were already delivering and poor schools were always inherently unlikely to be able to do so.

The prime minister's liberal social instincts seem to stop short at education where he has shown himself to be ferociously and even ignorantly reactionary, almost as if his hostility to the service is in direct proportion to his own lack of academic success.

From the Guardian, *June 1992*

They create a desolation and call it peace.
Tacitus recording a Caledonian chieftain's perception of Roman imperialism

It's all about learning

Learning is most often figuring out how to use what you already know in order to go beyond what you currently think.

Jerome Bruner

Minds are like parachutes
They only function when they're open.

Sir James Dewar

Ideas are free
We pay for *not* using them.

Anon.

When your mind goes blank
Don't forget to turn off the sound.

Anon.

Only the educated are free.

Epictetus

Only the truly ignorant
Think they know everything.
The wise have learned how to find out.

Anon.

If you think that the cost of education is high,
You should see the cost of ignorance.

Anon.

The easier it is to communicate
The harder it is to get anyone to listen.

Anon.

A single conversation with a wise man is better than ten years of study.

Chinese proverb

Learning is not compulsory... neither is survival.

W. Edwards Derning

Someday, in the distant future, our grandchildren's grandchildren will develop a new equivalent of our classrooms. They will spend many hours in front of boxes with fires glowing within. May they have the wisdom to know the difference between light and knowledge.

Plato on future learning (allegedly)

People love to learn but hate to be taught.

Michael Yacobian, internationally renowned trainer

The best learning happens in real life with real problems and real people and not in classrooms.

Charles Handy

The biggest obstacle to innovation is thinking it can be done the old way.

Jim Wetherbe, Texas Tech, 1990

Learning is not taught.

Nicholas Negroponte

If we don't focus on the experience dimension of learning, we run the risk of mistaking the publishing of information for learning and training.

Elliott Masie

You can't teach people everything they need to know. The best you can do is position them where they can find what they need to know when they need to know it.

Seymour Papert

It's what we think we know already that keeps us from learning.

Claude Bernard

In a time of drastic change, it is the learners who inherit the future. The learned find themselves equipped to live in a world that no longer exists.

Eric Hoffler, Vanguard Management, 1989

The most fundamental skill is learning how to learn. It's more important than subject knowledge because it's learning for life, not just for now.

Author

We need to bring learning to people instead of people to learning.

Elliot Macie

Before you become too entranced with gorgeous gadgets and mesmerizing video displays, let me remind you that information is not knowledge, knowledge is not wisdom, and wisdom is not foresight. Each grows out of the other, and we need them all.

Arthur C. Clark

Live as if you were to die tomorrow; learn as if you were to live forever.

M.K. Gandhi

Education is learning what you didn't know you didn't know.

George Boas

Genius is one percent inspiration and ninety-nine percent perspiration.

Thomas Alva Edison

Education is not filling a pail but the lighting of a fire.

William Butler Yeats

The mediocre teacher tells.
The good teacher explains.
The superior teacher demonstrates.
The great teacher inspires.

William Arthur Ward

In *Long Walk to Freedom* (1994) Nelson Mandela pointed out that education was the engine of personal development. He said that it is what we make out of what we have, not what we are given, that separates one person from another. In this way the child of a humble farmer can become president of the state.

Accounts of Eton beatings at
http://home.freeuk.net/mkb/
pubschool.htm

All Africa.com: http://allafrica.com

Arson Prevention Bureau:
http://www.arsonprevention bureau.
org.uk

Bentley, T. (1998), *Learning Beyond the
Classroom: Education for a Changing
World*, Routledge-Falmer

Blyton, E., The Famous Five Stories:
http://www.btinternet.com/~ajarvis/
blyton/five.htm

Board of Education (1993), *Syllabus of
Physical Training for Schools*

Boyson, R. (1975), *The Crisis in
Education*, Frank Cass Publishers

Brighouse, T. (1999), 'Home and
School', in *Modern Educational
Myths*, ed. Bob O'Hagan, Kogan
Page

British Educational Communications
and Technology Agency (Becta)
(2002), *ImpaCT2 report*:
http://www.becta.org.uk/research/
research.cfm?section=1&id=539

Boyson, R. (1975), *The Crisis in
Education*, Frank Cass Publishers

Brighouse, T. (1999), 'Home and
School', in *Modern Educational
Myths,* (ed.) Bob O'Hagan, Kogan
Page

Brog, W. and Voltenauer-Lagemann, M.
(1989), 'Germany', in *Delinquency
and Vandalism in Public Transport*
(pp. 25–72), Paris, European
Conference of Ministers of Transport

Brown, P. and Hesketh, A. (2004),
*The Mismanagement of Talent:
Employability and Jobs in the
Knowledge Economy*, Oxford
University Press

Buckeridge, A. The Jennings Stories

Butcher, J.S. (1965), *Greyfriars School;
A Prospectus*, Cassell

Chartered Institute of Library and
Information Professional (CILIP)
(2003), *Survey of Secondary School
Libraries*

The Child Accident Prevention Trust:
http://www.capt.org.uk/

The Child Bereavement Trust:
http://www.childbereavement.
org.uk/

Cook, V. (2004), *Accomodating Brocolli
in the Cemetary*, Profile Books

Crompton, R. The William Stories

Department for Education and Skills,
(DfES), Nutritional Guidelines:
http://www.dfes.gov.uk/
schoollunches/

Department for Education and Skills
(DfES), statistical website:
http://www.dfes.gov.uk/statistics/

Department for Education and Skills
(DfES), Trends In Education and
Skills
http://www.dfes.gov.uk/trends/

Department for Education and Skills
(DfES), (2003a), Statistics of
Education, Schools in England:
http://www.dfes.gov.uk/rsgateway/
DB/VOL/v000417/index.shtml

Department for Education and Skills
(DfES), (2003b), The 2003 England
and Wales Secondary Schools
Curriculum and Staffing Survey:
http://www.dfes.gov.uk/rsgateway/
DB/SFR/s000413/index.shtml,
25 September 2004

Department for Education and Skills,
(DfES) (2003c), Survey of ICT in
Schools:
www.dfes.gov.uk/ictinschools

Department For Transport (DfT)
(1998–2000), *National Travel Survey*

Department od Education and Science
(DES) (1975), *A Language for Life*
(The Bullock Report), HMSO

Dewey, J. (1897), My Pedagogic Creed',
The School Journal, 54:3
(16 January), pp. 77–80

Dick, W., Carey, L. and Carey, J.O. (2001), 'Analyzing learners and contexts', in *The Systematic Design of Instruction*, 5th edn, New York: Addison-Wesley, Chapter 5

Eisenberg, M.B. and Berkowitz, R.E. (1990), *Information Problem-Solving: The Big Six Skills Approach to Library and Information Skills Instruction*, Norwood, NJ: Ablex Publishing

Evans, GE. (1956), *Ask The Fellows Who Cut The Hay*, Faber

Famous dyslexics: http://www.garry.karen.btinternet.co.uk/famous.dyslexics.htm; http://maher.maddsites.com/dyslexia/

Ferri, E. (ed.) (1993), 'Life at 33' – the fifth follow-up of the National Child Development Survey

Fitch, J. (1897), *Thomas and Matthew Arnold: Their Influence on English Education*

Francis, P. (1992), *What's Wrong with The National Curriculum*, Liberty Books

Gee, H.L. (1938), *Every Boy's Book: An Epitome of Information Covering all the Interests and Activities of the Modern Boy*, University of London Press

General Teaching Council (GTC) 'census' 2002–3. Survey, conducted by MORI for the GTC: http://www.gtce.org.uk/news/news Detail.asp?NewsId=481

Hall, S. and Haywood, J. (2001), *The Penguin Atlas of British and Irish History*, Penguin Books

Hargreaves, D. (2003), *Education Epidemic: Transforming Secondary Schools through Innovation Networks*: http://www.demos.co.uk/catalogue/educationepidemic_page276.aspx

Hindmarsh, A. *et al.* (2004), The Times *Good University Guide*

International Telecommunication Union Report: http://www.itu.int

McBer, H. (2000), *A Model of Teacher Effectiveness*, Department for Education and Employment: http://www.teachernet.gov.uk/_doc/1487/haymcber.doc

McCrum, M. (1989), *Thomas Arnold, Headmaster*, Oxford University Press

Mandela, N. (1994), *Long Walk to Freedom*, Little Brown

Medicines and Healthcare Products Regulatory Agency (MHRA): http://mhra.gov.uk

Milliband, D. (2004), 'Personalised learning: bulding a new relationship with schools', speech as Minister of State for School Standards, North of England Education Conference, Belfast, 8 January, available at: http://www.teachernet.gov.uk/growingschools/support/detail.cfm?id=35

Moon, B. (1999) 'Ten fallacies associated with testing', in O'Hagan, B., *Modern Educational Myths*, Kogan Page

National Audit Office (2003), *Making a Difference: Performance of Maintained Secondary Schools in England*, November

National Education Statistics: http://www.statistics.gov.uk

National Federation for Educational Research (NFER) http://www.nfer.ac.uk/research/research.asp

Office for National Statistics (2002), *Social Focus in Brief: Children 2002*: www.statistics.gov.uk/.../social-focus-in-briefchildren/Social_Focus_in_Brief_Children_2002.pdf

Office of Arts and Libraries/Working Party on School Library Services (1984), *School Libraries: The Foundation of the Curriculum*, HMSO

Ontario Institute for Studies in Education (2003), *Watching and Learning 3*: http://www.standards.dfes.gov.uk/literacy/publications/research/63525/, 25 January 2004

Organisation for Economic Co-operation and Development (OECD): http://www.oecd.org/

Owen, H. and Bell, J. (1967), *Wilfred Owen Collected Letters*, Oxford University Press

Oxford information at http://www.oxford-info.com

Palmer, J. (ed.) *et al.* (2001), *Fifty Major Thinkers on Education: From Confucius to Dewey*, Routledge Key Guides, an imprint of Taylor & Francis Books

Peake, M. (1970), *Gormenghast*, Penguin Modern Classics

Qualifications and Curriculum Authority (QCA) (2003), *Curriculum 2000 Review*, phase 3 (December); http://www.qca.org.uk/

Richards, F., The Greyfriars stories, Magnet Comics; from 1947 Cassell

Rowling, J.K. (2001), *Harry Potter Paperback Boxed Set*: Four Volumes, Bloomsbury

Schön, D. (1973) *Beyond the Stable State*, Penguin

Scientific Advisory Committee on Nutrition (2003), *Review of Research on the Effects of Food Promotion to Children*, SACN/03/25, prepared for the Food Standards Agency by the University of Strathclyde: http://www.sacn.gov.uk/, 22 October 2004

Smith, A.P. (2000), 'Stress and health at work part V: factors associated with occupational stress', *Occupational Health Review*, 88, pp. 26–8

Smithers, A. and Robinson, P. (2000a), *A Life in Secondary Teaching: Finding Time for Learning*, Centre for Education and Employment Research, University of Liverpool: www.data.teachers.org.uk, 22 June 2004

Smithers, A. and Robinson, P. (2000b), *Teachers Leaving*, Centre for Education and Employment Research, University of Liverpool: www.data.teachers.org.uk, 18 December 2004

Social Trends 32: http://www.statistics.gov.uk

Spending Review UK 2003: http://www.dfes.gov.uk/2002spendingreview/

Taylor, K. (1994), *Central Cambridge: A Guide to the University and Colleges*, Cambridge University Press

Teachernet http://www.teachernet.gov.uk/supplyteachers/

The Teacher Support Network: http://www.teacherline.org.uk/

The 2003 England and Wales Secondary Schools Curriculum and Staffing Survey

The Times newspaper; also available at http://www.timesonline.co.uk/

Toffler, A. (1998), *Information Studies Grades 1–12*, Toronto: Ontario School Library Association, draft

UK 2003 The Official Statistical Yearbook of the United Kingdom and Northern Ireland: http://www.statistics.gov.uk/statbase/Product.asp?vlnk=5703&More=N

UNESCO (2001), 'Sub Saharan Africa', UNESCO Institute of Statistics

Watching and Learning 3. Final Report of the External Evaluation of England's National Literacy and Numeracy Strategies

WHO (2004), *Young People's Health in Context: Health Behaviour in School-aged Children (HBSC) Study*, international report from the 2001/2002 survey, eds C. Currie, C. Roberts, A. Morgan, R. Smith, W. Settertobulte, O. Sandal and V. Barnekow Rasmussen